LEARNING to LIVE Again

From ADVERSITIES To ADVENTURES

DOROTHY WILLIAMS

Copyright © 2021 by Dorothy Williams
All rights reserved.

No part of this publication may be reproduced, stored in a retrieval system, or transmitted in any form or by any means, electronic, mechanical, photocopying, recording, scanning, or otherwise, without the prior written permission of the author.

LEARNING TO LIVE AGAIN
From Adversities to Adventures

Dorothy Williams
learning2liveagain24@gmail.com

ISBN 978-1-943342-07-5

Printed in the United States of America
Destined To Publish
www.destinedtopublish.com

DEDICATION

I dedicate this book to my late husband, Gregory Williams. He will always live in my heart.

ACKNOWLEDGMENTS

I want to acknowledge my wonderful, supportive children, Cheryl, Christina, and Gregory Jr., who are my precious jewels. I'm very proud of their love and support.

Many thanks to my niece, Sabrina Pitts, who inspired and encouraged me to write this book.

REVIEW

Learning to Live Again: Adversities to Adventures by Dorothy Williams takes the reader on a journey through five chapters. The book opens with a captivating introduction that fuels the reader's quest to know more. It speaks a lot about the author in words that could galvanize questions like "What's next?"

The first chapter carries the biography of the author, demonstrating her exuberance and passion for what she does. This book journals her health issues. The weight of her health challenges is conveyed unambiguously to her readers and will stir emotions in their minds. The chapter goes forth to turn the tables around, using that heartfelt story to question the reader about discovering their true selves. It then teaches the reader how to deal with challenges, giving them the formula to do so. The chapter concludes with a charge: "Winners never quit, and quitters never win." The second chapter starts by teaching the reader that their circumstances doesn't define them. Among other themes, it teaches the art of moving forward and mastering a positive mental attitude. The third chapter ignites a heap of

Review

thoughts in the reader. It spurs reflection and motivates a desire to seek God's glory in uncommon ways. It also teaches about being intentional about yourself. The fourth chapter touches on the importance of maintaining a good perspective on life. It focuses on having a healthy attitude and reason that can help the reader grow and develop, and it also speaks about the author's adventures during the COVID period.

This book presents itself in a suspenseful, thrilling, story-like form that keeps the reader on their toes. The major themes of the book are self-discovery, the power of one's mind, and the importance of being surrounded by supportive people as you live every day. Without being pretentious with words, the writer is courageous, and the book is highly recommended for readers who are learning to live again in spite of adversity.

Dr. Barbara Brooks

TABLE OF CONTENTS

Introduction 1

Chapter I: In the Beginning. 5
    A. Discover Your Adventurous Self 11
    B. Do You Know the Real You? 17
    C. Love Yourself 21
    D. Dealing with Challenges in Life 24
    E. The Formula: Prayer, Faith, and Patience. 29
    F. Winners Never Quit and Quitters Never Win 31

Chapter II: Your Circumstances Don't Define You 41
    A. Making Up My Mind to Move Forward. 45
    B. Positive Mental Attitude 49
    C. Let Your Journey Begin. 56
    D. Embrace Other People 61
    E. Experience an Awakening. 63

Chapter III: How Would You Look Back on Your Life? . . . 69
    A. Reflection 72
    B. In Every Story You Can See God's Glory 76
    C. Finding Your Perfect Partner: You. 80
    D. Rekindle the Child in You. 83

Chapter IV: Keeping Your Adventurous Self Alive 91
    A. Learning to Live Again in the
       Midst of Life Circumstances 94
    B. Develop a New You. 98
    C. The Time to Live Unapologetically Is Now! 102
    D. New Perspective in Life 106
    E. Personal Transformation and Growth 110
    F. Adventures During the Covid-19 Season 116
    G. Reflections on My Adventures 120

Chapter V: Conclusion 123

INTRODUCTION

Writing this book came naturally to me upon realizing how God had blessed me to join the ranks of those who have survived a combination of deadly illnesses. I am sharing my experience in this book with the hope of encouraging you and helping you to know beyond a shadow of a doubt that you, too, can be victorious over dire circumstances. The contents of this book reveal how individuals can overcome what may appear at first to be impossible odds. I was in a challenging personal struggle. I was in a season where I wasn't sure I would survive to tell my story, until I decided that there was no other option—I would survive it. No, I would not just survive it; I would learn how to live again!

People deal with overwhelming situations every day and feel they cannot cope with them in their despair. Through my testimony, I offer some methods to counter the mental and emotional stress that can threaten to make one give up on life. When people are severely challenged, they often find their spiritual resources stretched to the limit. Yet in the face of adversity, we

Introduction

can learn how to get a grip and not allow fear to undermine our chance of success. In these pages, I strive to send a message to you that receiving bad news—of a medical or financial nature, for example—does not mean the end of the world, or the end of our dreams. Our hopes and dreams, along with our very existence, can and do survive any difficulty that comes our way.

I'm not trying to tell you that I woke up one day and decided that everything would be fine, and instantly all was right with the world. That's not how life works, and you know this, but with each test comes a testimony. I would like to share my testimony and the role my faith played in my success. There were times when I felt as though God had given up on me. "Life is not a bed of roses"—this statement became reality when life started caving in on me.

Bad things happen throughout life, whether trivial or severe. In telling my story, I won't be painting a pretty picture or sugar-coating anything for you. This was an ordeal with many ugly sides, and it was tough on both my body and my mind. I survived it, against all odds, although I thought many times that I would not. Through faith, prayer, and patience, and with God's help, I survived. My hope is that you can find motivation in the experience of my story—in pain, in joy, in adversity, and also in victory.

Thank God for my late husband, my children, and my faith, because now I can tell people how I got over. I learned to *live again*, and I have discovered my adventurous self. I decided from the beginning of my health challenges that I was not giving up. Oh yes, I had my moments. But overall, I knew I was not one to give up, no matter how serious the situation. I knew I had to make some serious decisions, and by placing my faith in God, many prayers, and patience, I knew He would see me through.

Introduction

I was also fortunate to have a supportive husband by my side, and a robust and healthy body throughout the prime of my life. I kept pursuing my interests and being passionate. In general, I believed, like so many other people, that "life begins at 40," and nothing could strike me down.

Learning to Live Again is a book about finding that certain something that will give you a personal formula for defeating self-doubt. Self-doubt comes to destroy our lives, our peace, and our safety. It comes to undermine our faith and trust in God. Why? Because if doubt succeeds at undermining us, then it can defeat us. I dedicate this book to those who want to come out of doubting and live victoriously.

This chapter in my life took time to navigate. I came across many bumps in the road throughout my ordeal. But I survived! I do not mean to sound like a broken record. Still, my life changed, my perspective shifted, and I learned more in this time about life and prioritizing myself than I ever could have imagined. Despite my circumstances, I learned how to *live again*, and in the process, I *discovered my adventurous self*, a part of me that I had never met.

In the Beginning

In 1994, I taught second grade in the Chicago Public Schools, living my passion for teaching and shaping young people's minds. My classroom was located on the third floor. Walking up the stairs had never been a problem—in fact, I had a bounce to my walk because I always had an exuberant amount of energy. One day, suddenly, I started feeling short of breath while walking up the stairs. After climbing just one flight, I had to stop to catch my breath before proceeding to the next level. This was very unusual for me. I thought to myself, "I really need to exercise more." By the time I reached the third floor, I was gasping for air and had to stop and rest for a minute to catch my breath again.

I have always enjoyed teaching my students how to sing in harmony and play songs on the recorder, and they would often put on performances for their parents. One day, while preparing

In The Beginning

them for an upcoming performance, I was demonstrating a song on the recorder. It only takes a small effort to blow air into it and make sounds. Yet again, this effort made me start coughing and struggling to catch my breath.

For years, I was a choir director at my church, and I enjoyed singing and playing the piano. One day, while I was directing the choir and leading a song, I started coughing, choking, and gasping for air. I had never had much trouble singing before, so I tried my best to compose myself, hoping that the symptoms would go away. But then some discomfort came over my body, and the symptoms kept getting worse every few seconds. Finally, I had to stop singing, and another soloist took over the song. I realized that I couldn't help it, yet I still felt very embarrassed.

Although I tried my best to maintain a healthy body, I still ended up being overweight. It became harder for me to catch my breath, even when I was only doing an everyday task that was not so demanding. Unfortunately, my condition got worse with time. As the days went by, I noticed other abnormalities, such as night sweats and frequent episodes of extreme perspiration, which soaked my nightclothes and bedding. Night sweats are usually related to an underlying medical condition or illness, but at that time, I did not know what was going on in my body, so I figured that I was just going through the changes of life with all the sweating.

Then, one day in 1995, my new beginning threatened to become my ending. It had become more difficult for me to walk up stairs at work and at home. I was only able to climb up three steps at a time before having to stop and catch my breath. Singing was no longer in the cards for me. I was not able to control my gasp reflex. I suffered embarrassment repeatedly, running off the choir

In The Beginning

stand, choking and gasping for air, and trying to make it to the bathroom to relieve the phlegm that came up in my throat from coughing. Suppose this had happened during the Covid-19 season—people would have certainly thought, "That girl has the coronavirus; let's get out of here."

After numerous doctor visits and all the medication to control the symptoms, the root cause of this illness still had not been determined. I was misdiagnosed with bronchitis and pneumonia several times and given antibiotics and inhalers that did not help. This went on for months without any alleviation from all the coughing and other symptoms. My chest felt like I had heavy weights sitting on it. I experienced a loss of appetite and found it extremely difficult to eat even a bit of food. I went from being overweight to underweight, losing 40 pounds within two months' time.

Something much more significant and harder to handle was in store for me, and somehow I knew it would not help if I ignored all of these symptoms. I never felt any satisfaction from doctors regarding all the changes to my body, and no one referred me to see a specialist during that time. I began to search for a doctor with more knowledge about my condition to receive the appropriate treatment. The process did not go as smoothly as I had hoped it would. I went from doctor to doctor and was repeatedly misdiagnosed. Later that year, my sister, who lives in Maryland, encouraged me to go to Johns Hopkins University Hospital in Baltimore. She made an appointment for me with a pulmonologist (lung doctor), where I was diagnosed with a lung disease called pulmonary sarcoidosis.

Sarcoidosis is a chronic illness that occurs in people all over the world. This chronic condition, thought to be an autoimmune disorder, is the most common of the fibrotic lung disorders; it occurs so frequently in the United States that Congress was led to establish a National Sarcoidosis Awareness Day in 1990. It causes nodules or granulomas to grow in any organ of the body, such as the heart, lungs, lymph nodes, kidneys, spleen, skin, bone, or nerves. Unfortunately for me, I was challenged with this in every area except the kidneys. The granulomas can usually heal and disappear on their own, but if they don't heal, the lung tissue can remain inflamed and become scarred and stiff, which was what happened in my case.

Prior to this, I had never heard of sarcoidosis. I was told that it is considered a mystery disease with no known cure. Fortunately, there are treatments that hold out hope for remission. However, the disease can cause symptoms to develop that come and go over the course of a lifetime. The condition can appear suddenly and disappear the same way. For most, it does not disappear; therefore, my prognosis was not good.

Autoimmune diseases are still very new in the world of medicine, and the treatment is generally still very experimental. This is the dark side of an autoimmune disease: your immune system becomes so overactive and "paranoid" that it starts attacking not only diseased cells but healthy cells as well. A common slogan in the world of autoimmune diseases is "I am so tough only I can beat myself up."

The sarcoidosis disease continued spiraling out of control through my body. I developed granulomas on my face that looked like lesions. I went to see a dermatologist and was told that the only way to remove them was through steroid injections in each nodule. I followed the procedure as suggested. After all, the face is the first part of what someone looks at, and the last thing I

In The Beginning

wanted was to draw more attention to myself. This procedure had to be repeated every six weeks to control all of the granulomas. It was a very painful process because there wasn't any numbing treatment given before the injections were administered.

Treatments for pulmonary sarcoidosis are generally done to control symptoms and improve the function of organs affected by the disease, and they work differently for different people. I was placed on 40mg of prednisone (an oral steroid) daily. Although it helped to reduce some of the inflammation, it did not completely cure my overall condition. I felt like I became an experiment using different drug treatments to control all the systemic symptoms. And then, finally, I was put on an even higher dose of steroids, 60mg, which caused more problems.

The doctor never explained to me any of the serious side effects prolonged usage of prednisone could cause. My muscles weakened, making it exceedingly difficult to accomplish the simplest tasks, such as dressing myself. Other side effects that I experienced were mood swings and difficulty sleeping at night, and I ended up with steroid-induced diabetes. Eventually, I developed osteoporosis: my bones were deteriorating. My body became frail, and I could no longer function like an average person throughout my daily life. I was told by two different specialists that I needed a right knee and hip replacement.

I became excessively overweight because of the prednisone and the lack of ability to exercise. My stomach became so enlarged that I looked like a pregnant woman getting ready to deliver. I went to several doctors because of the pain I was experiencing. I went to the emergency room twice, only to be given medicine for the pain. Finally, I was told that my spleen was enlarged. Every day it became even harder for me to walk and breathe while carrying all

In The Beginning

those extra pounds. I lost my senses of taste and smell for seven years without any known explanation.

During the time when I was suffering with this illness and serious side effects of all the medication, I continued working. I was still performing my duties as a wife, mother, and caregiver to my developmentally challenged brother and my elderly parents. Later, just when I thought it could not get any worse, I began dealing with heart arrhythmia, which was caused by the sarcoidosis. I was hospitalized several times because of my heart condition.

Since this disease had affected me so systemically, my husband helped to seek better treatment for me. We decided to go to the world-renowned Mayo Clinic, located in Minnesota. There, I was diagnosed with lymphoma, which is a general term for cancers that develop in the lymphatic system. The lymphatic system is part of the body's immune defense system. It helps maintain fluid balance in the body by collecting excess fluid and particulate matter from tissues and depositing them in the bloodstream. It also helps the body to fight disease and infection by supplying disease-fighting cells called lymphocytes. My body was already compromised with one autoimmune disorder, and now I had developed another. Eventually, I became oxygen dependent around the clock because I could no longer breathe effectively.

After consultation and intense deliberation with my physician at the Mayo Clinic, we decided that the best course of action was to have the enlarged spleen removed (a splenectomy), which I did at the Mayo Clinic in 1999. After the surgery, my doctor entered my room with a smile. He informed me that I'd lost a five-pound, three-ounce spleen, which was the size of a baby. He said, "Although you have lymph glands in your stomach which are the size of golf balls, after the removal and biopsy of one of them, there is no more evidence of lymphoma." The news sounded like music to my ears! The remaining sarcoidosis condition, by comparison, did not seem like such a bad sentence to live. My platelets went down in numbers, and I felt better.

I received three different prognoses during the duration of the illness: from six months to live, to only several weeks, and then, finally, the doctor told my family that he did not even think I would make it through the night. My immune system was shutting down. It was devastating for me and my family to hear such sad news. My husband was always there holding my hands, encouraging me that everything was going to be all right. By the grace of God, I survived and lived to see the next day. After I had my spleen removed, I started feeling better for the first time in years, although I was still dealing with physical challenges. Finally, I was going to get a break, at least I thought.

Going through all these challenges caused me to rethink my life and the course it would take. This is what a critical illness can accomplish in the life of a human being. It makes us realize that even in the midst of severe adversity, God will order our steps. Therefore, even when we are faced with dire circumstances, the Word of God says, *"we are more than conquerors"* (Romans 8:37).

DISCOVER YOUR ADVENTUROUS SELF

As I said before, I believed that "life begins at 40," as if there would always be more time, still another tomorrow. And why shouldn't we all feel this way? When you are young, you are invincible, bulletproof, and always ready for one more. In fact, this lesson can be shared with the youth. Time is precious, it runs

In The Beginning

out, and you should never waste any of it. We never know what tomorrow will bring.

I never knew I had so much desire for adventures pent up inside me. Although traveling was on the table, I thought about world traveling as something I would do after retirement. In my wildest dreams, I never thought I would love partaking in adventures like skydiving, getting into a race car and driving 138 miles per hour, or flying an airplane. I never considered myself a daredevil or adrenaline junkie. I discovered a girl I didn't know, a "new me." My strength, not my weakness, became my focus.

My daily purpose was to live life as an adventure—we should make it count. We shouldn't feel trapped in our monotonous daily routines and circumstances. Once you have the courage and confidence to live an authentic life and discover your adventurous self, you often don't have the youth, energy, and courage to go with it. But many individuals go through challenges and break the norms, and we are living in a time when all these norms and rules are being challenged and broken more and more often. Nick Vujicic, whom I admire, is a 38-year-old motivational speaker who was born without arms or legs. He has never allowed his physical disability to stop him from living his best life. His story of overcoming has inspired me in my own quest to live my best life.

I do not mean to sell a "pie in the sky" fantasy. An adventurous life comes with a balance of difficulties as well. Life is all about cause and effect. I believe it is important to note that you have the power to choose (realistically) which difficulties you would like to deal with. My adventurous self was not discovered until I was diagnosed with a life-threatening illness.

Later realized that I had become a stronger person during this period of my life. Through my adversity and suffering, I

In The Beginning

became more assertive in my spirit and developed into a fearless individual, no longer afraid to step out of my comfort zone to journey and try new things in life.

Discovering an adventurous side to yourself does not necessarily require you to start over again. Learn how to step out of your comfort zone by choosing to explore new things. Try some activities you have never tried or something that you have been thinking about doing. Try to develop some new habits.

So, with a deep feeling and an innate need, I started to pursue something I had always loved: singing and laughing. Both have a few health benefits, which is most likely a contributing factor to why I have always loved them. They are great stress relievers and mood boosters, and they release pain-relieving endorphins. I was no longer singing in the choir, but I started singing at home. An audience was not necessary. As far as laughing, I try to find humor daily by watching funny movies, listening to jokes, and sometimes just looking in the mirror and laughing at myself for acting silly. I am so thankful to be alive that I have learned to live every day as adventurously as possible, making sure it counts.

Why not break the mold of stagnation? At one point or another, each of us ends up feeling trapped in our same old daily routines and circumstances. Economists have called it the rat race, a term that has become famous because the metaphor is so powerful. In this rat race, days blend into each other, and each becomes more forgettable than the day before.

I realized that to achieve success, merely understanding the rules of society isn't enough. We need to find the true meaning of what we are doing, because the little things that happen in our lives could significantly impact our future. In finding this true meaning, we cannot use only our own knowledge and logic,

In The Beginning

because our capabilities are limited. We need to have something to believe in, something that can give us the strength to face many obstacles throughout our lives.

Living life with regrets is not something I want to look back on, especially in my golden years, wishing I had lived my life to the fullest. My husband encouraged me to start living my dreams despite the circumstances. He would always say, "Let's make some great memories." So, we did! I chose to learn how to live again. I chose life. The Word of God says Jesus has come that we might have life and have it more abundantly (John 10:10). So, I embraced His Word.

God has graced us with the power of choice—free will. We should appreciate this more often, but it can come with disadvantages. Unfortunately, some people can be blinded and mistakenly think they can live carelessly without much concern. Free will can be seen as a double-edged sword: it can be a good thing or a bad thing depending on the situation. On one side, it is good to have the freedom of choice in our lives because we can be open to abundant opportunities. But there is a lot of responsibility and effort that comes with that, so most people end up going with the flow of life.

I started out with small ways to break the mold of feeling sick every day. My husband played music, and I would dance sitting down. Soon, I was able to stand and dance around the house. One snowy winter day, I wanted to do something fun. I went into the yard, lay down in the snow, and made a snow angel with my body. I felt like a kid again.

My husband was very instrumental in telling jokes. Sometimes, they were not so funny, but I would laugh anyway. He tried so hard to make me laugh in many ways. He played every humorous

In The Beginning

video he could get his hands on to make me have a hearty laugh. He was definitely not a singer, but I gave him brownie points because he tried hard to amuse me. One day, he started singing "Moon River" by Andy Williams over and over again. The next day, the same song. He kept singing this song for days on end. Finally, I asked him, "Why do you keep singing this song?" The following weekend, he told me to pack my suitcase because we were going on a road trip. He kept me in suspense until we reached our destination: Branson, Missouri. Of course, we visited Andy Williams's Moon River Theatre.

It is essential for each of us to find our own way to be adventurous. This is something that cannot be forced on anyone but that comes from being more open to the world around us. There are many things that we still need to do, like meeting new people or experiencing different types of food. Think about the opportunities that you still need to take. Before we take our first step in this journey, it is also essential for us to recognize ourselves from within.

One day while sitting on the patio, I started pondering about places I wanted to visit. In fact, I made a list of places in the state and internationally. My husband encouraged me, saying, "Let's make it happen." In 2000, we flew to Rio de Janeiro, Brazil. Although I was very excited about going to Brazil, I experienced a lot of anxiety. Family members and friends kept telling me that I had to be crazy to take that type of risk to fly. I was already having trouble breathing, and flying at a high altitude, my oxygen level would be more compromised. I would have to use oxygen on the plane. They constantly reminded me of what could happen in flight, but I decided to take the risk because my husband, who was my biggest encourager, was right there by my

In The Beginning

side, and he constantly reminded me about exercising my faith. Today, you can bring your own FDA-approved portable oxygen on board, but personal oxygen units were not allowed on flights until 2005. So, in order to use oxygen on the flight, I had to pre-arrange and order it in advance through the airline. This was my first flight using oxygen. I had to practice meditation in flight to keep the rhythm of my breath steady, making sure I would not hyperventilate from anxiety. Also, I played gospel and meditation music through my headphones for encouragement to help me relax during the flight.

Brazil

Learn to start living today.
We never know what tomorrow may bring.

In The Beginning

DO YOU KNOW THE REAL YOU?

I did not know the real me—especially the adventurous side of myself. For most of my life, I allowed myself to fit in the mold society had made for me as a woman. I did not have a true identity of my own. I spent much of my life wondering and worrying about what others thought of me, as if their approval mattered.

Setting boundaries with others didn't come naturally to me. I felt like my parents raised me to serve and care for people. I didn't see examples of self-care in the home. I grew up letting others dictate who I am. Since I did not set my boundaries, others set them for me. Trying so hard to please other people, I forgot that my feelings were important too. People will take advantage of you if you allow them to. It took time, but I learned to let go of anyone who made me feel less than the person I am. Today, I have no trouble saying no gently, unapologetically, with no explanation. Too often, we try so hard to please other people and forget that our own feelings and dreams are important as well.

Have you allowed yourself to discover who you are and what you truly love? Who you are becomes exposed when adversities come your way. There is a lot of literature on this, but most of it is only possible to digest with specific life experiences. The bottom line is, when you are your true self, you are not worried about other people's opinions of you or approval of your actions.

"Knowing yourself is the beginning of all wisdom." – Aristotle

You cannot be what God has intended for you to be if you are continually checking for others' approval and permission. You were created with specific character traits, passions, and talents for a reason, so you should enjoy being fully yourself.

In The Beginning

The process of becoming comfortable with yourself and discovering who you are starts with self-evaluation. Take some quiet time to reflect on who you really are and not what others want you to be. Don't compare yourself to other people, such as images of celebrities in the media, or people on social media who pretend to be someone they are really not. Sometimes, we aspire to emulate them, but to learn the real you, you must start learning your true passions and calling. Often, we allow our dreams to be influenced by culture, media, and exposure around us, rather than taking some time to think over the actual priorities that lie within us.

I decided to start getting to know the real me. Truthfully, there should not have been anything keeping me from getting to know myself earlier. I think it is just a privilege that comes with age, something I wish to pass on to the youth and teach them to do while they are young and brave: learn to be comfortable and confident. Too many children are burdened with insecurity, self-loathing, and doubt, and are unable to love and trust themselves at a time in their lives that is so powerful and transformative. This behavior can go into adulthood without self-awareness, which is what happened to me.

"Being yourself" can be something of a challenge, as most of us have had a lifetime of managing other people's expectations concerning who we are, what we think, and how we behave. Being the person you want to be can involve showing the many parts of you that you may have kept hidden, You may start expressing ideas and opinions that are dear to you, but that you have kept quiet about, and making choices of all kinds concerning people and things. Being you reveals to the world that you have something unique to offer, which can take courage. It can feel like you are

In The Beginning

starting all over again and rewriting who you are. Everything to this point has shaped who you have become, and much of it may still remain hidden. I believe we are molded by our failures, as much as by our successes: nothing is wasted. Don't you think you owe it to yourself to let your unique light shine brightly? It would be so sad to think that you feel the need to suppress all that makes you who you are. I would encourage you, even if it is little by little, to start celebrating who you are and sharing that gem with others.

One of my favorite movies is *The Shawshank Redemption*, starring Morgan Freeman as Big Red. Tim Robbins starred as Andy Dufresne, who was framed for killing his wife and sentenced to life in prison. One statement that stood out in the movie to me was when Andy said, "Get busy living or get busy dying." Andy chose to live and broke out of prison. Although he was physically in prison, mentally, he was not. How many times do we stay a prisoner in our own mind… just going through the motions in life? I broke free of my prison mentality of being afraid to follow my dreams.

I made a conscious decision to acknowledge that I had not lived my life to the fullest, and I would not continue to live my life afraid, worrying about whether I would see my next birthday. I started living mentally. I wanted to spread my wings like an eagle. My spirit felt like that of an eagle, so I wanted to fly like one. In fact, that is why I decided to take a skydiving adventure, to experience the feeling of spreading my arms like an eagle, not figuratively but literally. Skydiving is what I started dreaming of—so, why not make it happen? It became one of the items at the top of my bucket list.

In The Beginning

Wow! Can you imagine willfully jumping out of a plane? I can honestly share with you how free I felt! The biggest adventure of them all.

When you are your true self, you are not worried about what other people think of you. When you truly know yourself, you have the freedom to live a life that you want, a life that serves you and prioritizes the things that make your soul soar.

Learn to soar and broaden your horizon.

In The Beginning

I have no regrets, and I'm glad that I decided to take on this experience for myself and no one else. Skydiving made me feel alive again! Talk about adrenaline, wow! It was thrilling to look upon that beautiful view. And I had no difficulty breathing. While soaring through the sky, I had the best time of my life! I made funny faces for my photographer, made dancing gestures with my instructor, and surprised myself by feeling completely at peace within myself.

We often allow our circumstances and life situations to keep us from living and to dictate who we are. By discovering your true self, you will find that the sky is the limit for anyone who is daring to soar.

LOVE YOURSELF

Learning how to embrace and love myself did not come easy. I often felt so embarrassed because of all the weight gain from high doses of steroids (prednisone). Some people I knew expressed that they didn't recognize me. Eventually, I started wearing long skirts and dresses, trying to cover up. I walked with my head down to avoid looking at people staring at me with pity. Many times, I found it challenging to look at myself in the mirror. My hair became so thin and frail-looking from all the effects of the medication that I kept it covered up.

When I looked in the mirror, I no longer recognized myself. The skin lesions on my face caused disfiguration. I went to a dermatologist every six weeks to have each nodule injected with steroids to keep them under control. The high doses of oral steroids made my shoulders look like a football player's, and the weight gain was a significant factor.

In The Beginning

My self-esteem took a beating because I no longer had the ability to do my usual activities. Now, I was forced to rely on my husband and children for help with simple things. I was no longer able to work and function in the same capacity.

Eventually, this illness made me feel so bad that I thought others didn't want to be around me. I realized later that I had stopped loving myself due to feeling inadequate from feeling sick and weak all the time, not like my normal self. Throughout my life, loving others was emphasized more than loving and embracing myself, so self-love was something I had to learn.

During this time, I discovered that I had many hidden issues that had never been dealt with. While I was meditating, God revealed some of them to me, and I could no longer run from them. As a child, I was raped by a so-called public, trusted individual, a police officer. I was only 16 and had never been with a guy. This act caused me to go into a state of numbness. My coping strategy to survive this ordeal was to hide inwardly and act as if nothing had happened. During that time, I felt uncomfortable talking to my family about this crime against me, so I suffered in silence. After all, the police officer told me that no one would believe me.

I was not aware of the effect this rape had on me until I was in my 40s. One day, my son announced to me that he would like to become a police officer, and the same feeling of numbness came over me. I collapsed on the sofa at the thought of it. It was then that I realized I needed help. It became obvious to me that this was one of the reasons I had trouble loving myself. The shame of feeling dirty had such a significant impact on my life. This man, who took a part of me away, severely damaged me emotionally for years.

In The Beginning

For a period of time, I fell into the trap of feeling "less than" others because of my emotional and physical challenges. My self-esteem took a beating. Illnesses or other struggles can lead to a form of self-rejection. When we berate ourselves for our weaknesses, we reject who we are and our capabilities. When others hurt us or reject us, it is much more significant because we have created vulnerability through our self-rejection.

There is great value in starting over, no matter what age you are, what you have lost, or how long you have been dependent on other people. Taking responsibility for my own life and my decisions presented many more challenges to my worth. Still, by working through the challenges with God's help, I gained a greater sense of worth than I had ever enjoyed previously. I found a new me!

To stop putting myself last was a hard lesson to learn. Now, I put my health and well-being at the top of my priority list. This way, I can be healthy enough to help others who need it whenever I can, without feeling the burnout I used to experience. Eventually, I came to accept and love myself for who I am and not allow my circumstances to define me. I had to learn how to love myself despite my flaws and insecurity. Finally, I was able to look in the mirror and tell myself that I am beautiful!

In The Beginning

Learn how to fall in love with yourself and start living again.

DEALING WITH CHALLENGES IN LIFE

Although challenges are a part of life, I came to the conclusion that I was only existing and not living my life as I should. An essential thing for life is our ability to breathe. We cannot spend more than even a short time without it. I lost my ability to breathe effectively without the aid of an oxygen supplement. Also, I had a nebulizer machine to help me breathe better and a CPAP machine to keep my airways open while sleeping.

In The Beginning

Eventually, it got to the point where I couldn't even go upstairs. Numerous times, the paramedics had to come because I could not breathe. In the meantime, waiting for them, I was still gasping for air. It was very frightening not knowing whether each breath would be my last, so it was very debilitating. Trust me. It was devastating.

Sarcoidosis caused me to lose my sense of smell and taste and diminished oxygen flow to my brain. This, coupled with all the medications I was on, often led to confusion and forgetfulness. This was the perfect storm, as I started forgetting meaningful tasks such as attending to food on the stove. Since I could not smell, the smoke from the burning pot would often go undetected. I remember one instance when the smoke alarm somehow malfunctioned and, thankfully, one of my neighbors smelled the smoke coming from my house and called the fire department. At that time, I was at my lowest. Before I could resolve one problem, another one followed. My husband even had to childproof the house just for my safety, which made me feel like I was losing my independence. It even got to the point where I could no longer drive.

Being on such a heavy dose of prednisone made me feel psychotic at times. Sometimes, I would see visions of things that weren't there. At roughly the same time, I started experiencing excruciating pain throughout my body. It felt like a bolt of lightning was shocking me. The pain was sometimes very unbearable. Many times, I couldn't control the urge to scream, which scared my family. I was a sight to be around.

One of the most excellent tools a person has at their disposal is encouragement. When hopelessness sets in, people naturally

In The Beginning

engage in self-pity. Some self-pity is to be expected, but we are not to linger in it too long, or it will become an emotional trap.

It is not beneficial for anyone going through an illness to be in the company of people who feed on their condition. Therefore, it is necessary to guard your associations and make sure you surround yourself with people who encourage you, not those who feed into your feelings.

From the very beginning, people who are ill need to be allowed to grieve over the loss of their health. It is also okay to be angry; this is part of the grief process of coping. However, anger is destructive if allowed to fester and spill over into our relationships with the people we love, especially family. Nor does anger contribute to healing the body; instead, it is toxic to the system. For a short period, anger colored my overall outlook on life; this is why prayer is so important.

Only someone who has "been there, done that" can know what it is like to hear a group of doctors tell you that you will live such a short time and know that, back at home, you have beautiful children depending on you. The very next thought is, "If something happens to me, my husband will be alone with a heavy load." My thought after that was, "How are my children going to respond and cope with having a mother who may not survive?" Not knowing at the time exactly how my illnesses would progress, I had at least been told enough to know that my children may have to face some devastating news about their mom.

At the time of my diagnosis, my husband and I had a daughter in college, a daughter in high school, and a son in elementary school. In some ways, I was like a "supermom": alert, energetic, and always on the spot for my family. I will not go as far as to say we were "Ozzie and Harriet" or "The Brady Bunch," but our

In The Beginning

family was somewhere in the realm of that stereotype in many ways. I was the dutiful wife. Since my mother's passing in 1993, I had become a caregiver to my brother, who is developmentally challenged from a childhood head trauma.

So, how did my family react? Let me say that, as for myself, I was in control to a certain extent. I had a good handle on maintaining my responsibilities and obligations to my family. My children did not realize how ill I was. Looking back, some of them were in denial. However, overall, my children were tolerant, although they did not fully understand why their mother had suddenly become so ill. A lot had to be going on inside their heads, but none of them showed anger or bitterness. I do thank God for my children.

My husband, Gregory, rose to the cause. He did not even seem to mind. Without fuss or fanfare, my husband did for our children what I was not able to do for them when I was at my worst. He faithfully took me to all my doctors without fail. This included our trips out of town so I could see medical specialists. It also included going on vacations when I really needed a break to change the scenery.

Now that my children are all grown and have matured in many ways as adults, they have relayed to me that they were amazed at what I went through. I was touched to know that they were paying attention and learned how to be strong from me. Also, my children witnessed how my husband and I cared for my mother, father, and brother over many years. I am sure that all of what they saw from their father and me will last them a lifetime. My children knew that no matter what was happening to me health-wise, I was still their mother who loved them dearly.

In The Beginning

Today, I am so proud of my children. All three have turned out to be fine individuals, with goals, dreams, and a sense of responsibility toward life overall.

My children saw me suffer physically, mentally, and emotionally. They learned first-hand that life has its ups and downs. They eventually saw visible demonstrations from me of coping, surviving, and being grateful for life, regardless of my circumstances. It allowed them to translate their love for me into action and become more caring.

Learn to allow your circumstances to hold you back in life. Remember that God can see you through.

In The Beginning

THE FORMULA: PRAYER, FAITH, AND PATIENCE

I lost heart many times during this ordeal. It may sound dramatic, but imagine your body that has always been strong and dependable suddenly letting you down, popping up with pain and illness around every corner, and no matter how hard you try, you simply cannot get to the bottom of it. Even though it did not make sense for me to feel this way, I often felt betrayed and did not understand why all of these awful things were happening to me.

We do not have that much control over our own lives. We are simply trying our best to strive and keep living in this world filled with unexpected ordeals. It was only when I reached rock bottom that I could finally understand the reality of my situation. The fact is that we are very weak and fragile. But it does not have to end there. One thing that remained true and steadfast throughout all of this was that God was on my side. If it weren't for prayer, faith, and patience (trusting in the Lord), I would not have made it through this test to be able to deliver this testimony.

During this time, there were several Bible verses that came to light for me. This verse stood out the most: *"Trust in the LORD with all your heart and do not lean on your own understanding"* (Proverbs 3:5). I definitely did not understand why all of this was happening to me.

Whenever I was going through an episode I wasn't sure I could handle, I was reminded that I wasn't doing this on my own, so I clasped my hands and closed my eyes in prayer and trusted that God knew how this would turn out. I would be reminded of the scripture, *"Consider it pure joy, my brothers and sisters, whenever you face trials of many kinds, because you know that the testing of*

In The Beginning

your faith produces perseverance" (James 1:2-3). In all honesty, I found no joy in the suffering. But I knew I had to keep the faith and wait for my healing.

I often prayed for God to get me out of the situation. By exercising my prayers and my strong faith, I made it through with God on my side. People, in general, can find many ways to overcome their problems while believing that they deserve all of the credit. But what they do not understand is just how little an impact they can truly have on their own lives—might as well call it a gamble. The way that I overcame the illness, God got the glory.

It requires tremendous strength to see a situation through when every fiber in your being is screaming for the problem to be over, or for it to change as soon as possible. Patience is a virtue. I want to assure you that if you just take a few deep breaths, break down your situation into manageable pieces, and trust in your faith, you will overcome any obstacle.

This formula—prayer, faith, and patience—is a recipe for dealing with any situation. Suffering, pain, and obstacles are all relative to the time and place in which they are happening. No one person suffers more than another; everyone has obstacles and hard times they need to get through. Using this formula, you can conquer anything. Knowing you will make it through will not necessarily make it any easier, but with your faith, you will become a tough warrior.

In The Beginning

Learn how to dive into the unknown. Remember to take a few deep breaths, break down your situation into manageable pieces, and trust in your faith. Through prayer, faith, and patience, you can overcome any obstacle.

WINNERS NEVER QUIT AND QUITTERS NEVER WIN

Believe you can do it! Whatever it is, you must first believe you can do it. That was the situation I was facing when I considered going back to school to get my doctoral degree. Having so much self-doubt ingrained in me, I had to overcome those negative beliefs and believe I could do it. You hear people say all the time, "It's all about timing," but even though the timing did not look good for me, it did not matter. I was on the outside feeling an inward determination. Other people had no hope of understanding the full weight and measure of what was going on inside of me.

In The Beginning

To other people, I picked a fine time to think about going back to school. After all, I was seriously ill, and I knew it and others did too. My diagnosis was not encouraging, and my prognosis was bleak. As far as pursuing something like a degree, that was completely out of the question—or so they thought.

I was determined to challenge myself. This would mean having to defy my doctors, family, and friends. However, I had to follow my inner drive and strike out into unfamiliar territory. Although I had experienced going to college, I was going to be a "challenged" student this time, which was new to me. Therefore, I knew ahead of time that it would not be easy.

The effects of my illness on my mind and body meant that I had lost the ability to concentrate or focus properly long enough to accomplish certain tasks. Even reading and doing homework was not going to come easy. After all, I had problems with my eyes and a short attention span due to chronic pain and fatigue. I had to start from scratch, learning to do things such as taking notes and engaging in critical thinking. On the creative end of things, I had lost some ground because of the emotional toll my health challenge had taken on me. I was creative, all right—creative in terms of trying to figure out how to get well. Needless to say, my confidence had plummeted as well. I was somebody who was used to being in control of my faculties and my surroundings. Now, I had to depend more than ever on my husband. He was the one who encouraged me to go for it. He assured me that he would do whatever he could to help me succeed.

Going back to school with a serious health challenge as baggage was more than a notion. My self-image had suffered a setback, and I had to build back my confidence before I could ever hope to be successful. I was pursuing my doctorate in education, and I

In The Beginning

knew I would encounter classmates from all walks of life, mostly professionals in their own right. I was aware of the fact that people are not always sympathetic to the plight of others. For me, that meant people would be judging me, and these same people would be my peers. Talk about peer review! Here was an opportunity for me to ward off feelings of inadequacy and intimidation.

The thought of being under a microscope did not sit well with me at first. I knew my professors would be monitoring my academic performance very closely. To build my self-assessment, which was the most important of all, I had my feelings to consider. I had to approve of my performance, to say the least. I did not want to get bogged down in wondering if I had made a mistake or bitten off more than I could chew. I knew that I was about to go out into the deep if I pursued a doctorate at this time in my life.

I had my doubts, but I did not let them overpower my determination. After all, I would be confronting a lot of personal fears. And it wasn't like I had a fan club cheering me on. My husband was very supportive from the moment I made up my mind to go for it, but others were concerned about whether or not I could stand up to the physical and mental challenge. I had decided I did not want anyone to feel sorry for me. I wanted to hold my own. Thank goodness I had another person besides my husband who gave me encouragement and a great deal of moral support. I had a friend there if I needed someone to talk to. And I encouraged myself by leaning on the Lord.

At first, I felt like I was on top of the world in the doctorate program. I met new friends, overcame my fear of failure, and developed some stability in my life—or so I thought. Just when I gained a sense of normalcy, the sarcoidosis raised its ugly head again.

In The Beginning

I started developing uveitis (inflammation of the middle layer of the eye), which affected my vision, making it even harder to see words. The symptoms of uveitis include redness, pain, light sensitivity, blurred vision, and dark floating spots in the field of vision. It can be severe and lead to permanent loss of vision, so as you can imagine, my nerves were growing even rawer at this point.

Stress is a typical vicious cycle for autoimmune conditions. The stress of having an invisible illness causes more immune system aggression, meaning that your immune system starts attacking the body even more. The only way to treat the inflammation from the uveitis was to use steroid eye drops. If you are counting, I was already on two separate sources of steroids to keep my symptoms under control, and now I had started experiencing very excruciating pain in my eyes. As a result, another doctor had to be added to the list. He informed me that the uveitis was a result of the sarcoidosis. Now, while in school, I had this new health issue to deal with. I was feeling so overwhelmed that the thought of quitting came to mind.

Some interesting discoveries came out of an otherwise trying time. I learned the importance of patience. I thought I would have to admit defeat and quit the program, but I learned that there were so many resources available for people who were experiencing vision loss. One source in particular allowed me to get most of my books on tape. Also, I used a tape recorder in class instead of having to take notes, and a classmate volunteered to assist me when needed. Finally, I realized I could resume my studies in a new way to accommodate my visual changes.

We must stand in the face of dire circumstances and hardships, no matter how bad things look. It is never about what things look like now, it is about what is around the corner, for that is where

In The Beginning

you will find success. As the saying goes, "Winners never quit, and quitters never win." The R&B recording artist Billy Ocean came out with a record some years ago with the oft-quoted line, "When the going gets tough, the tough get going." How true! In my own personal experience and in life as a whole, I try to stay focused on being tough and *not giving up*.

I had a rude awakening when I could no longer take the skills I was blessed with for granted. I spent many years trying to achieve my level of education, but during those earlier years, my health had never been an issue. My finances were never as taxed, and my self-confidence was not something I had to reinvent. Up to this point in my educational journey, I never had to guard my life, because it was not in jeopardy, at least not from a health crisis. Nor did I have more people trying to discourage me than cheering me on. Returning to school in the midst of health challenges was an exhilarating yet crucial time in my life. I had to be very strong, very focused, and steadfast in my faith. On one level, I felt like it was me against the world. I had to believe I could do it, and I did it! The rest is history.

I completed the doctoral program in 2005, after five years of study. For me, it was not about the title, it was about the winning attitude I had to sustain long enough to reach the finish line. It was about setting an example for my children and for others who have serious health challenges and have to push themselves to climb that mountain. It was about me being able to demonstrate by example that if you believe you can do something—whatever it is—you can.

Pursuing my doctoral degree was about far more than getting another piece of paper. I was looking forward to being able to tell young people, especially disadvantaged youth, what they, too,

In The Beginning

could accomplish despite the odds against them. Now, I can be bold when I encourage others to defy the odds, because I have done so myself. Now, I am reminding others that they can do the same. Although I had taught children with disabilities before, I have now learned first-hand to live in their world physically and mentally.

My academic adventure enables me to say to a seasoned individual, "You're never too old to go back to school and finish with flying colors." Age is just a number. Now, I can say to those who doubted my sanity and my tenacity, "See, I wasn't crazy after all." I can say to them now, "If there is something you have been holding off doing, don't put it off any longer." I knew back then that tomorrow was not promised, but that is true whether you are sick or in perfect health. When you are given only a short time to live, or when you've been written off by a doctor or two, it is even more imperative that you ask yourself, "Whose report are you going to believe?" That is straight from the Bible (Isaiah 53:1). Now, I understand how important it is to ask yourself that question in trying times and respond with the right answer: "I am going to listen only to a praise report!" That means I am not going to hear, see, or speak evil, death, or defeat. I only see God's promises up ahead.

Do not be afraid to sniff out the opportunity to move beyond your circumstances. Yes, there were times when the going got rough. However, I held on and persevered. There is a saying, "Nothing wins out but perseverance." In other words, the person who makes it to the finish line does so because they do not give up. Therefore, don't give up! Don't quit! Stay the course. The rougher it gets, the more determined you must become to stick it out. When it looks like you're going to fall, keep standing. When others make snide remarks and laugh at what you are doing, just look past their ignorance and envy. Pray for them, that they may become enlightened and see the error of their ways. In the meantime, remember that much of what we endure is not only for our own growth and development; it is also designed for us to use our testimony to encourage others to be the best they can be. In this way, our trials and tribulations are not endured in vain.

Last but not least, I rest easier knowing that I challenged myself at the worst possible time in my life! By the grace of God, I survived what was an ordeal, an emotional roller coaster, a daredevil experience, and a test of courage. I remained alive to experience a medical miracle: I went back for my doctorate and it did not kill me. In the end, I threw a victory party.

Today, God has blessed me to be an inspiration to my children and others. I encourage you, before you take off on your journey, not to forget the formula: prayer, faith, and patience. Don't give up on your dreams.

People graduate because they have taken certain courses in school, learned their lessons, done their homework, and maintained passing grades. In other words, they have satisfied the requirements of the institution and its curriculum. The school of life, of which man's schools are also a part, requires us to strive to learn the lessons we are being mandated to learn. In order to graduate in life, we must master each level of experience, and then we will be released to embrace the next set of lessons. Just like in the schools that society sets up, we must do our homework. We must come to know first-hand the knowledge and tools it will take for us to get out of life what we are here on earth to learn. God has His own requirements, and we must meet them. God's curriculum requires that we learn how to have faith and be obedient to His

Word, which equips us to meet life's challenges and pass the tests set before us.

I knew that I had graduated when I looked up and, against the backdrop of all that I had experienced and gone through, I was still here—still breathing, walking around, and talking; still setting goals, hoping, and dreaming; still praising God, worshiping, and eventually passing on the torch. God did it, not me! It was not because of anything I did. So, I give Him all of the glory, honor, and praise.

To those of you who have yet to graduate from your most pressing challenge, the message is, "Hold on. Don't give up. Know that God is able." Then go on to fulfill the graduation requirements of life.

To those who are reading this book and are about to go across life's stage, I pass the torch to you. Congratulations! And to all, I say, "Be encouraged. Continue to walk in victory!" Remember that, "winners never quit, and quitters never win."

In The Beginning

Learn that the race isn't given to the swift,
but to those who finish the course.

11

Your Circumstances Don't Define You

Your life can be changed for the better and for the worse. Sometimes it can be predicated on your attitude toward situations and how you handle them. Much of life is beyond our control, but we can choose how we handle life's circumstances. I felt deep within that I wanted to live, and I tried to fight for it. I know that ultimately, God has the last word. He didn't put in my spirit that He was finished with me.

I survived the challenge of being ill because I kept my mind on creating an innovative approach to survival. Why not? Either I would give in to my condition and prognosis, or I would fight back. Perhaps it was because I was an educator that I thought about turning my situation into a personal learning experience.

Your Circumstances Don't Define You

However, this idea did not come to me initially—I had to discover how to cope in new ways. I had decided this, and I knew God would help me through it. My family and I had faith, and together, we would move mountains. It was not some miracle turnaround, though. It was the beginning of my recovery and the beginning of a long and mentally challenging journey.

When I reflect on how far God has brought me, I am so grateful that it causes me to weep. There was a time when it took all of my energy just to go to the bathroom. If you haven't experienced this, you can only imagine the incredible and debilitating fatigue that individuals living and dealing with chronic illness go through. It takes days to recuperate from an energy-draining activity.

When you are living with a chronic illness, some people's expectations do not change. They cannot comprehend the depth of your illness, and they still expect you to be there for them in the same way as before, especially your family and friends. They expect you to be as you used to be and how they have always known you to be.

The woman that my family and friends knew was no longer the same. I realized that I could no longer be there for others. I had to focus on taking care of myself in order to reserve my energy and survive my circumstances. I refused to let it define me.

Ultimately, I developed a strong will to live and decided to fight for my life. I asked God to allow me to live to see my children finish school and to see my grandchildren, and He did just that. I am a living testimony. It all started with a decision to move forward. I decided that I would not remain in this position; I would move beyond the current circumstances and move forward to experience my abundant life.

Your Circumstances Don't Define You

I knew I had a lot more living to do. I had a family who loved me—and an adventurous life to live. God granted me the desires of my heart. I lived to see all of my children complete college, and I have two beautiful grandchildren.

We all have different stories, and we all face various adversities. Whether physical, emotional, or spiritual, the challenges are real. But those challenging circumstances do not define us. It's a matter of choosing whether you will let your circumstances define who you are, or whether you will define your own future. Remember that you are stronger than you think. I learned on a daily basis how to challenge myself to take control of my circumstances and to try not to allow them to control me.

Some of life's happenings are beyond our control, and how we respond can sometimes be the key to the outcome. My experience has also revealed to me who I really am versus who I thought I was. It was not until I had faced life-and-death issues that I realized my own level of faith in God (or lack thereof). The illness really tested me on all levels. A demand was placed on every internal and external resource I had or thought I had. There was a lot of learning for me during this time. Through it all, I did not allow my circumstances to define me.

One morning in Sunday school, I was asked to read a Bible passage, and I couldn't read it. I felt like a child in kindergarten trying to sound out the words. I felt like I was being undressed and all of my underlying issues were now exposed. At that moment, I felt helpless.

Many times, while I was teaching class, I would experience difficulties recalling my students' names. My short-term memory skills were so challenged that I could no longer teach effectively. It also became challenging to walk because of the excruciating

Your Circumstances Don't Define You

pain, which I believe was due to my prolonged use of prednisone. Eventually, I had to leave my job, giving up my passion for teaching, which was heartbreaking. Although I have always worn a smile on my face, I was hurting inside, feeling defeated.

It took a lot for me to give myself the grace to know that none of the challenges I was going through defined me as a person. My life always had a significant amount of value, and it still does. Don't allow circumstances to hold you back. You don't have to let your circumstances represent you—you can define yourself, and the best way to do this is by getting to know yourself.

Learn never to let your circumstances define who you are.
You can do anything if you put your mind to it.

MAKING UP MY MIND
TO MOVE FORWARD

One very popular Chinese proverb says, "The journey of a thousand miles begins with the first step." Well, my first step was to *believe I could* take that first step! My personal adventure began with a made-up mind—a made-up mind that I would not give up on life and I would not give up on getting well, even though sometimes it looked like I was at death's door. I made up my mind at the beginning of my journey that I would not quit! Don't you see? It was my mind that was made up—I wanted my adversities to turn into adventures.

Maintaining a positive mindset and exercising patience are extremely critical in order to move forward in life. As I struggled with my challenge, there were more bad days than good. What I *did* was learn to remain patient with myself. Sometimes God will bring people to the point of acceptance. During a certain phase in the middle of a crisis, regardless of its nature—physical, financial, or emotional—there can be more bad days than good. Therefore, it is only through patience that we can persevere and sustain ourselves ("stand," as the Apostle Paul spoke of) until the number of good days surpasses the bad. There is always a breakthrough waiting around the corner. There was a drive in me that would not allow me to give up!

We all have experienced our own pits in life, where we have felt stuck and unsure about how to move forward. Sometimes it was not our fault at all, but a few situations were the result of poor choices that we have made. On other occasions, the choices of others have adversely affected our lives.

Your Circumstances Don't Define You

As for me, I am a very practical person, and I have always believed that certain people connect with you seasonally or throughout a lifetime for a reason. By talking to others about my experiences and my emotional turmoil, I can help them in some way, not just to overcome strife in their lives but also to push them toward personal growth and building a better life for themselves and the people who depend on them. I do not believe that your circumstances dictate the final outcome; your choices do. It was my choice to engage in adventurous activities in the midst of my challenges to make my life more exciting. I did not want to wait until my life was completely back to normal. Making the most of my time and my life became my biggest priority.

I genuinely think that believing you can do something is half the battle. It is like anything else in life: you do not fully know what lies ahead. However, with a determined attitude, you can step out in faith. Regardless of any prior knowledge about the context, there are still unanticipated challenges, obstacles, and potholes awaiting you. There are issues, incidents, and problems that will arise, and you cannot be prepared for them because you do not have a clue what is around the corner.

As Joyce Meyer says, "Do it afraid." This is a statement that I embraced figuratively and literally early in my life. Often, I would feel hesitant about jumping into things that I really wanted to experience in life. Fear would curtail my enthusiasm as I began to worry about the risks involved. Now, I realize my greatest risk is not learning how to move forward in life and how to avoid staying stuck, because we know that life is not going to wait for anyone. There is a great, wonderful, adventurous life waiting for each one of us. We must step out of our comfort zone to grab hold of it. Life is the ultimate choose-your-own-adventure event.

Your Circumstances Don't Define You

And since none of us are getting out of it alive, why not choose the most epic adventure? Why not choose something that feels right for you?

One of the best ways to diminish fear is to branch out when the time is wrong, not when it is right. You see, many people never do what they want in life because they are always waiting for the "right time." If I had kept procrastinating and using my physical challenge as an excuse, afraid to move forward, I never would have started to experience my best life. The right time to move forward in life is now!

Watching NASCAR racing on television was always a thrill. I got caught up in a moment and I began visualizing myself driving a race car. One day, I decided to make it happen. Why not? I wanted to enjoy the experience of driving a NASCAR car race. After engaging in thorough research about race car driving, I decided to venture out so I could actually live in the moment and experience driving in the fast lane—"Wow, I was behind the steering wheel of a *real* race car!" Not once did I reveal this to the people I knew; surely, they would have thought that I was losing my mind.

In everyday life, my driving speed is average. However, I wanted to get a taste of what it feels like to be in an actual NASCAR race for fun. Although I had not driven a stick shift car since I was a teenager, I decided to step out of my comfort zone and do it anyway.

Although I was somewhat anxious at first as I was stepping into the unknown, I slowly overcame my fear. A surge of energy came over me. I was able to accelerate my car to a high speed as I steadily drove past the other drivers and moved into the fast lane of the racetrack. For some reason, I became hyper-focused behind

Your Circumstances Don't Define You

the wheel. My competitive spirit soared high, and out came the daredevil in me! I reached a speed of 138 miles per hour. As I climbed out of the car later, I realized what was happening. I felt extraordinary. The spectators on the side appeared enthusiastic and excited, making a lot of noise and clapping frantically to cheer me on. I felt like a rock star, high up on a pedestal. I was the only female, and I believe I was also the oldest driver out there. I could not believe that I was able to pull off this adventure without practice. Talk about a daredevil experience. What an adrenaline rush! I did something I wanted to do to stir up that adventurous spirit in me. I was able to do it while afraid and move past my fears.

Life has so much to offer, and I was glad to embrace the opportunity to move forward and enjoy it!

Your Circumstances Don't Define You

Learn to embrace what life has to offer. Make up your mind to move forward and choose to enjoy what you love in life.

POSITIVE MENTAL ATTITUDE

I knew I had the desire and the will to live. So, it was vital for me to cultivate habits that accompanied the fortitude of a positive mental attitude. Even if you are someone who has never estimated the depths and the difficulty associated with mental strength, it is in times when you have no choice that you discover the strength that God has instilled in you. Searching for a silver lining is crucial if you are stuck in a dark situation. On some days, this attitude could be the difference between life and death, and you wouldn't be able to survive the day without it.

A chunk of my life is already known to you by now, but there is more to learn. Earlier on, a positive attitude was a coping strategy to live. If I was going to survive, my attitude would need to be tuned to demonstrate the fact that I *wanted* to live. It is not always so simple to stay positive or optimistic, and it was tough for me to maintain this attitude toward my life when I was so ill. It was challenging and terrifying to have to deal with such uncertainty in my life, especially not knowing whether I would wake up the following day or not. I was devastated and struggling to breathe, and I experienced excruciating pain daily, which was very difficult for me to deal with. My life was spiraling out of control. Surrendering to the doctors and what they said—that I did not have long to live—was one of the most challenging phases of my life. With this thought persistently pecking at my brain, how could I keep a positive attitude?

I felt like I was stepping into the unknown. For a while, I was petrified and had a tough time coping with all that was happening to me. I definitely didn't feel upbeat during that time, mainly because there was so much uncertainty involved.

I learned to wear a smile on my face and to keep cheering, parading a positive attitude as if it were a cape. First, it was my coping mechanism for survival, but later it became my reality. It really helped me navigate through some very tough times. While experiencing acute episodes of excruciating pain, I would tell myself that it would be okay. I began looking at the brighter side of life.

Thoughts are like videos that play in your mind over and over again. As the Bible says, *"Ask and it will be given to you"* (Matthew

Your Circumstances Don't Define You

7:7). It is important to ask for the right things. So, play the right video repeatedly in your mind. At some point, you will have repeated the positive message to yourself and those around you so often that it becomes a reality in your mind and soon a fact in itself.

A positive mental attitude can be likened to faith, although faith has a stronger, unwavering foundation. This reiterates the fact that God has a plan and that everything happens for a reason. However, the fact is that your attitude can shape your life and mold it into what you want it to be. Remember, your attitude matters. Only God knows the part of the story written on the next page of your life, and you can only accept it as it is, because you can't erase or rewrite it. However, carrying the right attitude can impact your life in positive ways. Attitude alone may not provide solutions to a problem, but it may help guide you toward one. It makes life bearable, if nothing else.

In the past, I tried listening to some family members and friends who were very healthy individuals, and most of them had never dealt with a life-threatening illness. Although I knew they accepted this reality, they tried to encourage me, and their hopes resonated with ideas such as "everything happens for a reason." I was used to hearing comments like, "I'm sure that you will be strong from going through this" or, "Hey, God knows best." I felt pressured just to put on a smile. During that period of life, I didn't know how to cheer myself up, because I didn't *feel* cheerful. I felt like screaming, "You're not the one who's going through this, it's me." They never saw me in a new light or understood that I could not do all of these things, because I didn't sit around complaining to them about what I was going through. Naturally, they expected me to help them through their difficult situations just like the old me, not realizing that I was not able to live up to their expectations anymore.

There were many things I used to enjoy doing that I was no longer able to do. I was used to being in control, and it took me a while to get to the stage where I learned how to focus on and deal with what I could still control. I became more proactive with my health. I began to watch what I ate and researched healthy foods to aid in my healing. This became my new norm.

Eventually, I learned that it was my belief that I had control over all these aspects of my life. I decided to watch my diet and become more proactive with a healthier lifestyle. I had a choice. I built it for myself. I started doing research about things that affected me and learned more about my psychological ability.

My go-to person was my husband. I could honestly pour my heart out to him, and he always found the right words to say. I felt so uplifted by the time my husband finished listening and talking to me. He was my trusted confidant. He was there for me every step of the journey, and I felt very blessed to have him in my life. However, I needed someone else who could tolerate hearing me talk about my feelings so that I could relieve my husband a little, so I sought help from a therapist. Not only was she a great listener, but she also had an upbeat personality. After leaving the office, I felt upbeat too. I came to realize that having the right attitude is essential for my well-being.

Now that I had realized the importance of attitude, it changed things. Eventually, it started to change my perspective and beliefs about my circumstances. By changing my attitude, I could grow past my struggles (over which I had no control anyway). I was no longer a victim of my circumstance but was the victor over them. This was a real rocky road; I had to learn things that I had yet to be exposed to earlier. For example, I learned about the power of meditation through a friend who was a great meditator. I had never practiced it before, but during that stage, I was willing to try any healing modalities to make my life better, so I finally did. I went to a facility to learn how to meditate and gained conscious control of what was on my mind. It helped me a lot; I was able to focus more on the present instead of letting my mind wander toward my past. This is what brought about awareness and helped me handle my emotions in a healthy manner. I became more conscious and redirected my focus instead of letting my mind wander all over the place.

Often, during difficult circumstances, I would make it through the day by leveraging my positive attitude. I would tell myself repeatedly, "I am healed." There is a scripture in the Word of God that says, *"Call those things that be not as though they were"* (Romans 4:17). I began to embrace this during those trying times.

The longer I live, the more I realize the impact of attitude on my life. I knew in the beginning that my attitude was more important than any factual information that was thrown at me. The doctor had said that I did not have very long to live, but I stopped letting that information change my attitude toward life. I didn't buy into all that—no man had that kind of power over me. I had to look beyond it, because I believed I had a strong will to live.

Although life was very painful and stressful to me, the thing that helped me the most was having a clear mind and listening to the right words and guidance. I had moved past the circumstances that haunted my head and taken on a more positive attitude. My attitude was my welcome change, as my fitness and the physical challenges I had endured became catalysts that transformed me into the person I am today. I became strong and focused on genuinely living each day and appreciating what I had on my plate.

I decided to hang a poster in my bedroom with my picture in the middle and affirmations all around it. They declared, *I am a winner; I am grateful, peaceful, adventurous, fearless; I am an overcomer who is strong and confident.* Slowly but surely, I began to see myself in that light.

With these affirmations dominating my daily life, everything started to line up. My whole perspective about my situation changed: I wanted to live instead of throwing in the towel. So, by developing those positive affirmations and depending on God, my health condition changed.

Although I was still dealing with the same circumstances, my mindset changed. I just repeated the affirmations: *I am going to live!* That was when my spirit began coming to life. I stopped worrying about my prognosis and whether or not I was going to die. My mind was focused purely on living and making the most of my life. This was the first time in a long time that I really felt alive. Instead of having a pity party, I stopped overthinking and worrying. Internally, I felt so different. This change in my mindset gave me a whole new perspective on life. I started thinking about things I had never really paid attention to before. I didn't worry about what I couldn't do. Instead, I just stimulated my mind and told myself that I would do this. I started feverishly formulating various plans, many of which involved things I never thought I would do. That's when I started living, and I somehow managed to turn the tables around for myself. This was the life I was designed to live. This was my destiny.

I would advise you not to wait too long to learn what I'm learning. This experience has matured me in ways that seemed unimaginable. I believe that one of the keys to healing is in your attitude, as it was in mine—it changed my whole world. I am aware that every situation is different, but this was my experience, and these were my results. This change in my attitude had a ripple effect on my life and my family. All the people who knew me began to see a different version of me because I became cheerful and very optimistic about life. I learned how to celebrate life during that time more than I ever had before. I began to throw parties at home, and my house was known as the party house, or the house of celebration. God helped me to change my attitude, and that's when my world became a better place.

There are many benefits of cultivating a positive attitude. It can heighten your energy, increase your inner strength, inspire others, and give you the courage to deal with difficult challenges. For me, it made me want to start living again. This has improved my quality of life and decreased my stress levels. Also, looking for a silver lining made me better able to cope with my trial.

God gave me the joy that *"surpasses all understanding"* (Philippians 4:7) through my trial. If you want to fill your life with happiness and strong relationships, experience moments of continued success, and feel joy through every event, you need to hold on to a positive attitude. People who are content don't seek the best of everything. Instead, they make the best of what's available to them and seek contentment in everything they have and do. Attitude is what really matters. I did what I enjoyed: adventures!

Your Circumstances Don't Define You

Learn how to feel joy by cultivating a positive attitude!

LET YOUR JOURNEY BEGIN

We take almost everything wonderful in our lives for granted. Since I decided to choose life, I have learned to be grateful for the small things. The ability to breathe, walk, get dressed, process information, enjoy the sunrise—the list goes on and on. My sense of gratitude was heightened for small things I had never thought about before. How easy it is for us to take our blessings for granted until we lose those abilities. Of course, we will be grateful for answered prayers and important things in life, but what about all the little things, too? How often have you noticed the beautiful sunrise? My spirit became heightened for all the small things in life I used to take for granted. The truth is that I survived this test and gained a powerful testimony. But there were many occasions when I was unsure if I would pull through and wake up the next day. I thank God each morning for a fresh start to enjoy another day, which is something I never did before I was challenged. Thank God for His mercy. To Him I am grateful, and to Him I give the glory and honor for sparing my life.

Life is filled with challenges. It was a challenge for me to have the will to make a comeback and re-enter life's mainstream after all the attacks on my body. It was a massive challenge when I decided how to redirect my life, because with trauma comes side effects. You become more careful or wary, and you can view small things as a potential death sentence, so you must train yourself to be brave and adventurous again. I was unable to live a vibrant life for a long time, so I began a journey to becoming adventurous.

Here is where you can start living your adventurous life and getting to know your authentic self. If you're going through a challenge, when you begin returning to everyday life, make sure that you start looking at living a more fulfilling life for yourself, one that makes your soul sing. If you love to sing, as I do, and you want to start getting back into normal social activities, join a choir if you go to church. Try a karaoke night with your partner or friends, or simply put music on and sing around the house. I had to start giving myself permission to do everyday activities without worrying about the consequences of a reality when I was at my worst self. It was a journey of having to learn to live fully again. I did not jump straight into a full routine of everyday activities but started slowly with more manageable things.

Traveling has always excited me, and when it gets more adventurous, it is more interesting. When I was ready, I decided to begin a new journey in life to explore more international travel—a journey that has now become my new norm. I have decided to be willing to take chances in life by exploring new places and meeting people from different cultures. Being adventurous not only allows me to enjoy life, but it also allows me the feeling of being able to live in the moment. This experience has also rejuvenated, restored, and replenished my inner being. My life has changed for the better and is now more enjoyable.

Try something new! You do not even have to do it alone; you can also invite your friends or family members, as long as you find it enjoyable. Being more open to other interests might also be a good thing. It would not hurt for you to try new things and see if you like them. It may turn out that you love it! And if not, so what—at least you gave it a try. Make the decision to stare fear in the face and say, "I am going to do it!" The thing is, you will not know if you like an activity until you have tried it. I would never have found out that I was an adrenaline junkie with no fear of heights if I had never discovered that adventurous side of me. YES! I do consider myself to be an adventurous girl at heart!

To me, being adventurous simply means getting out of your comfort zone. Whenever I do the things that I normally don't, that's adventurous to me. I will try most things at least once before I pass judgment. There have been some adventurous activities I won't try—for example, while I don't have a fear of heights, I won't go mountain climbing, because I know that I am challenged and have some lung restriction, so I will not put myself at risk in that way. And I forgot to mention claustrophobia—God, please don't let me get stuck in an elevator! My understanding of being adventurous has dramatically changed in my life. I'm ready and willing to try any fun things that life has to offer.

As I have said, God has brought me a long way. During this time, God and His Word sustained me. Also, my personal goal-setting and organizational skills made an exceedingly difficult situation more manageable. I am still learning what this life is all about, but I know one thing: no matter what the challenge is, it is better to start over than to give up. There is great value in starting over, no matter how old you are, what you have lost, or how long you have been dependent on other people. The process of taking responsibility for my own life and my decisions has presented many more challenges to my sense of worth. Still, by working through the challenges and with God's help, I gained a greater sense of self-worth than I had ever enjoyed previously. By not giving up, I have been able to start an exciting journey in life.

For me, life is meant to be an adventure. The range of possible thrills and spills at your disposal is limited only by your imagination and the choices you make. You are not too old. You are not too young. You do not need a lot of money. You do not need to wait until you are older or wait for a better time. Right now is the only moment you ever have. So, let your journey begin!

When I was in high school, my aspiration was to join the Air Force to become a pilot. That dream never came to pass, but I realized it was never too late. I took a few flight lessons and lived to experience flying a plane.

Your Circumstances Don't Define You

I felt like an actual pilot navigating the plane. To help my journey along, I learned how to do some new things and praised the small and significant accomplishments.

Learn to fly. "The sky is the limit."

EMBRACE OTHER PEOPLE

I don't know about you, but I love meeting new people, having the opportunity to hear about their lives and adventures, and going to new places and trying different foods. Being around people who have similar interests can be incredibly beneficial, which can open your eyes to additional possibilities in life.

Some of my fondest memories have come from meeting new people while traveling. I have the best memories of traveling, being open to new friends along my journey, embracing the different personalities, and laughing together. I have found laughter to be a universal language.

From time to time, we need to rely on other people. While we can handle many things ourselves, we still need that social aspect in our lives. However, we also need to realize that everyone is unique and different from each other, so they will not all treat us the same way. Our brother or sister might be friendly and understanding, while our best friend might be more energetic and fun to interact with. These traits are not necessarily mutually exclusive, but they are usually somewhat distinct; for example, there are some secrets that you could share with your best friend but not with your brother or sister, even though both of them are friendly to you.

As we grow older, we can usually understand the fact that not everyone is perfect because we all make mistakes occasionally. We also need to know how our relationships with other people can influence our behavior and even our personalities in some way. I try to engage with like-minded people so that we can be an inspiration to one another. Since I love traveling, I seek out and go to places where people enjoy the same things I enjoy. I have

Your Circumstances Don't Define You

met many people from different cultures, ethnicities, backgrounds, and walks of life that I have remained in contact with to this day.

There are some people I may never be best buddies with, but that doesn't mean I don't want to spend time with them or don't value who they are. Not every place I have been was pleasant, but I still found ways to embrace the differences. I did not like every new food I have tried, but I did try them instead of assuming I wouldn't like them. If I always gravitated toward those things that I felt "safe" with, I would have missed out on some wonderful experiences and fascinating and incredible people. So, may I suggest that we all open our eyes from now on and notice the diversity of people and things around us? Embrace it, experience it, and decide whether you want to do it again.

Start finding some new things that you enjoy. Find a form of exercise that you want rather than feeling like you are torturing yourself. Go to the gym to find a new acquaintance. Go walking—you will be surprised who is on your path. Take long strolls with your friend or children or a hike through a nature reserve, and you will feel peace and tranquility. I learned how to ride a bike again and enjoyed every minute of it. You will be surprised by the new things and new people that are waiting for you to enjoy.

Enjoy laughing with friends. Listen to inspirational music and talks on podcasts and videos. Use the adversities you have endured as permission to live a life that serves you, that makes you happy and joyful in life.

Some of the best times I've experienced were with new people I didn't know, but we had commonality together. It allows you the opportunity to connect and create some fun memories. When I started enjoying and embracing new people in my life, my life became more enriched.

Your Circumstances Don't Define You

Learn how to enrich life by embracing new people.

EXPERIENCE AN AWAKENING

Have you ever had a light-bulb moment in life where you have been struggling with something for a while and suddenly realized that you had overlooked a simple and feasible solution to your problem? I consider this an awakening experience, where simple answers were there all along but were overlooked.

One night at church during a New Year's Eve service, people were sharing their testimony. A lady shared her testimony of being healed from stage four cancer. While she was giving her testimony, I was literally on the edge of my seat. I had been diagnosed with stage four sarcoidosis. She had also struggled with a critical illness, but she looked like she had never been sick a day in her life. She looked like the picture of perfect health.

Your Circumstances Don't Define You

After the service, food was served. I was so intrigued by her testimony that I seized the opportunity to introduce myself to her. I asked if I could contact her later, explaining that I was going through something similar to what she had experienced and telling her how amazed I felt that she had conquered the illness. It was a real blessing to get to know this courageous young woman. She told me she went to a naturopathic doctor who helped her change herself from the inside out. He informed her that she needed to change her diet right away in order to start her healing process. He explained how the body needed live enzymes to heal. Listening to her testimony undoubtedly inspired me, making me feel more empowered and giving me hope that I, too, could survive my health challenge.

The very next day, I called Dr. Williams to set up an appointment. Although I had heard of this philosophy of healing, I had never taken the time to learn about it. After being told numerous times by physicians that the medicine was keeping me alive, I had been hesitant to try more alternative methods. But now that I had reached a place where I was so burned out from trying so many different medications recommended by doctors, I decided to give this modality of healing a chance, especially after listening to her testimony. I felt like the lady in the Bible with the issue of blood—going from place to place, spending money, looking for answers and ways to heal my body.

During my appointment, we talked for over two hours. Dr. Williams tested me, assessing how serious I was about getting well. He informed me that I must make drastic life changes, especially with my diet. I must drink lots of water to keep my body hydrated, and juicing had to be a big part of my diet. He then set up a healing plan immediately.

Your Circumstances Don't Define You

When Dr. Williams informed me that health challenges could be reversed, he had my full attention. He told me about the importance of colon cleansing, commonly known as colon therapy, which removes toxins from the colon. He said that he would give me the tools and work with me to reverse the illness and help me to control and improve my quality of life. He said that we must first address the condition itself, not only the symptoms but what caused it. The goal was to help my body return to health.

The doctor emphasized drinking fresh juice and water daily. I know it sounds crazy, but I was desperate. I went to Dr. Williams several times for health education. Within three months, I felt like a new person. I couldn't believe how my body had started to feel alive again. I regained mental clarity and my ability to walk and climb stairs without pain. I never would have believed this could happen if I hadn't experienced it first-hand.

Later, he added exercise to my regimen. He taught me the importance of strength training, which would enhance my quality of life. This was done for one hour, three times weekly. Over a few months, I felt more and more strength in my body. Speaking of a transformation… I began to feel so amazing! Now, I could walk up the stairs with a bounce as I used to do in my earlier years.

Dr. Williams encouraged me to learn and practice yoga to improve my strength and flexibility, which I was struggling with during this time. I had never learned yoga before, and now I would be given yoga classes weekly. He taught me all the health benefits that I would receive from practicing yoga, and he demonstrated all types of poses that I would learn and eventually do.

I thought to myself, "He must be crazy. How can my body become that flexible?" All those moves that he demonstrated—shoulder and headstand—were out of the question for me. I could not visualize myself doing them. He assured me that I would be able to push past my body's limits over time and that I must practice daily at home.

I would not be truthful if I said the treatment plan was easy, because it took some hard work and some time to heal, but now that I am on the other side, I am thrilled and beyond thankful that I went on this journey. It had been years since I felt this good. Being able to climb stairs without gasping for air was huge. Juicing made me feel energized, and the episodes of sickness began to cease. I have rarely been sick with any colds or flu since I changed my diet. I struggled for such a long time before changing my diet that I didn't know it was possible to feel this good. I can now move my body with much flexibility, which is something I used to think was a thing of the past.

In addition to healing and coming off medication, I appreciate how I was given tough love as a patient. Dr. Williams's honesty and firmness held me accountable for myself, which I needed because his method encouraged me not to give up. He took the time to really listen to me. Although he was super caring, he wouldn't allow me to throw in the towel and give up on myself. He was very firm with his regimen.

Dr. Williams was a great motivator. He always spoke the right words at the right time to encourage me when I felt like giving up. Finding someone who cared this much and took the time to listen and offer so many holistic modalities to heal was rare on my health journey. The exuberant amount of energy I eventually felt was most definitely worth the time and effort it took to heal.

Working with Dr. Williams has been such a huge blessing in my life! Before meeting with him, I struggled for years and years and was always told that there was no cure. This was the first time in years that I had felt this good—feeling alive without the use of medication. (This was my level of faith; I would encourage anyone else to speak with their doctor before doing something this extreme.)

Soon my blood sugar stabilized, my high blood pressure went back to normal, and the sarcoidosis went into remission. I got my life back again by simply changing my diet and following Dr. Williams's regimen. As I learned how to live again, I experienced an awakening to the fact that my former food choices and eating habits had been causing havoc in my body.

I decided to celebrate my 66th birthday by taking pictures on the lake. Feeling on top of the world, I decided to do my yoga headstand. It was terrific feeling good and being flexible.

There was a time when climbing stairs was so hard that it made me struggle to catch my breath, and when life turned my world right side up again, being agile felt awesome!

Thank God for my ability to learn yoga. I was able to be flexible in my body in ways I never dreamed I could. As of today, I am still practicing yoga daily.

Your Circumstances Don't Define You

"Learn to look at life differently." An awakening experience can make you feel on top of the world.

III

How Would You Look Back on Your Life?

There is a gospel song I used to love singing that says, "As I look back over my life and I think things over, I can truly say that I've been blessed, I've got a testimony."

I've had the opportunity to enjoy the things that really mattered in my life. I enjoyed great moments with my children while molding them through their childhood to become productive adults. My family has always been my priority throughout my life. I'm grateful I stood the course of being married for 40 years. My husband and I enjoyed holding hands, being in each other's company, laughing together, rejoicing, and being happy with the path of life we shared together. Each journey of life was a stepping stone that stretched us to grow together.

How Would You Look Back On Your Life?

When you reflect at the end of life, what would your life say about you? What things did you accomplish, and what legacy is left behind? What type of impact did you have on family members and other people? Whose lives did you touch? Are you leaving a positive contribution to this world? Will you be significantly missed by your loved ones? I believe all of these questions are important to ponder. In fact, one of the reasons I am writing this book is to leave it as a legacy to my children and future generations.

Life is short and full of unforeseen circumstances, so we should strive to leave a positive mark behind. We can effect changes in our communities and our households—are we going to be able to look back on our lives and see that we have left a positive mark? Life should not be spent wasting valuable time, because time is one thing we know money can't buy. Don't be one of those people who look back at the end of their life and wish they had made better choices and done things differently. Some people feel obligated to family and society, instead of living a life that is true to themselves. I've witnessed, first-hand, loved ones who wished they had done things differently in their life, but time had run out for them. They wished they would have had the courage to do the things they wanted to do.

You are the one who must decide that the right time cannot be put off forever. Sure, there is such a thing as timing. But it is that inner clock along with prayer that tells you if you are telling time correctly. Do not let other people make the decision for you. If you do, it's like another person telling you when you need to go to the washroom. You get my drift? If it feels right, then do it. Who better to know when you need to purge than you? Embrace time, don't waste it.

How Would You Look Back On Your Life?

Adversities in life can force you to look back and weigh all your decisions. It is best to have as little regret as possible. It would be a pity if you were to look back and feel like there was more for you to do. It is vital to start living your best and most adventurous life as soon as possible. Start living today. Learn how to take more risks, play outside of your comfort zone, sample the richness of life, and leave no room for regrets.

Looking back, I'm glad I took the power of choice to step outside of my comfort zone to live my life adventurously. I chose not to leave room for regrets in my life. Going through my many challenges made me become a much stronger individual.

Learn to have the courage to do the things you would like to do in your life, so you will not have to live with regrets.

How Would You Look Back On Your Life?

REFLECTION

One of my favorite books is *Jonathan Livingston Seagull* by Richard Bach. There are many similarities between my life and that of this fictional character, a seagull who sought to defy mere existence in his search for freedom. My encounter with a life-threatening illness inspired me to adopt a new view of life. My challenge led me to search out the meaning of life as never before. In my quest to find answers, I, too, realized that a kind of freedom existed that I had yet to experience. I realized that my desire to have the kind of freedom that Jonathan Livingston Seagull found truly defied what so-called average people think of as possible.

My brush with death caused me to look at life with a level of reflection I had never known prior to my challenge. It was during this phase of becoming more aware that I discovered there is a type of freedom that most people never realize exists. I became like the seagull that achieved a high level of awareness in his present existence. By embracing this new level of consciousness, I began to soar in my spirit.

I had to flex my wings and muscles. My need for strength, just to stay alive, was real enough that I was now being driven by something deep within to get more out of life than ever before. It was as if I was living a paradox. There I was, sick as could be, yet more determined than ever to get more out of life! Jonathan Livingston Seagull was not confronted with a life-threatening illness like I was, but he was confronted with a way of life that is not transcended. A life that would leave him just ordinary. In other words, he would never achieve anything extraordinary. He had to be determined to soar beyond the limits that were placed on him, no matter what others thought. He did not conform to his world. In my world, it is not commonplace to attempt to rise above the ordinary, especially when you are ailing. People in perfect health are often satisfied with their mundane existence. Sometimes they do not reflect upon what more they can do with their lives, outside of what society has prescribed.

Jonathan Livingston Seagull bucked the establishment, shall we say, as far as his bird culture was concerned. In my own case, I started thinking "outside of the box" as I thought about what life really had to offer. In my health crisis, I realized I had never questioned the extent of my own existence, especially to the point of comprehending that life had much more to offer me than what I had experienced up to that point. Sometimes it takes being at death's door, or some other traumatic event, for us to have an "out-of-body experience." In my case, it wasn't literally an out-of-body experience, but it was an "out-of-the-box" experience. My condition was influencing my perception, which in turn was altering my thinking, which led to me taking action on a physical level I had never dreamed of taking.

I was very inspired by *Jonathan Livingston Seagull*, although my own story is what propelled me to write this book. I became restless. Something was stirring up deep down inside of me. This stirring inside overcame my fear of dying; it overcame any notions that I would not make it. All of the suffering during my illness was not in vain, because it caused me to question the extent of life's possibilities.

I came to the conclusion that I was being tested. If God was testing me, I was determined to learn everything I could about my condition so I could fight back! At that point, I wanted to pass the test no matter how difficult it was. I started surfing the internet to learn as much as I could about my health—listening to tapes, learning about others who had gone through similar experiences. What protocol did they take? I spoke with other overcomers and discovered how they had handled their health challenges.

I had to learn how to have peace and be content during my storm. Everyone has their own way of finding peace. We do not have to go away to meditate peacefully; we can find peace in the comfort of our own homes. This healthy lifestyle is what will keep our sanity in check throughout our daily life.

Spiritually speaking, I knew I had to put my faith and trust in God. I made up my mind that I was going to get myself through this, and my ordeal was not in vain. In the final analysis, I would have the victory and God would have the glory. I wanted to be able to help others help themselves, because if there's one thing about life challenges, it's that they make people feel helpless. I began using my profound knowledge to present workshops in various support groups to encourage people who were dealing with similar chronic conditions.

I also found someone who could listen to me on a daily basis. That someone was my husband, with whom I could express my pain and disappointment. He played a significant role in my healing. His encouragement gave me strength.

I know I am no longer the same because I am still here after being given three prognoses for how long I had to live! With all the medication, a host of medical tests, and treatments prescribed by the doctors involving powerful prescription drugs, I often became discouraged, but I never gave up hope. I am active to this day because I created a wellness plan for myself and became diligent in working on it. Setting goals became a high priority and one of the best things I had ever done. Thank God!

How Would You Look Back On Your Life?

It was hard to go from feeling like I was on top of the world one moment to my whole life beginning to change in the next moment. I realized that the blessings from adversity would come quicker if I was willing to go to the next level. I knew I could not remain where I was, in the state of mind where the illness placed me. I had to relinquish my ego to be able to move beyond my condition. I allowed my Heavenly Father to take charge of my life and situation by putting my ego in check. In other words, I surrendered to the Lord so that He could do for me what He said He would do, which is to "fight my battles," because the battle is His anyway.

How Would You Look Back On Your Life?

Learn to follow your dreams,
don't be afraid of embracing the moment.

IN EVERY STORY
YOU CAN SEE GOD'S GLORY

Now, looking back at my life, I can see God's glory in my story. I had an opportunity to witness how God's massive glory could manifest within me during the period of my challenge battling for my life. Throughout my many years of sickness, God's help and His glory were apparent. With no cure and no solution, there was only time and space for spiritual care. It became apparent that medicine alone would not address it.

At this point, I began constantly adding to my bucket list of things to do right away because God had given me renewed spirit. Through His grace, I was more hopeful than I had ever been, knowing I would live because I now had the confidence

How Would You Look Back On Your Life?

that God would bring my body back into balance. I began to feel the presence of His peace and strength in my heart consistently throughout my challenge. He has given me peace in the midst of my storm—a peace that no one would be able to understand unless they had been in my situation.

I realized that it was my mother who was my mentor. She taught me so much about life, and so much about overcoming adversities. Her life was a living testimony of God's glory! It was not just the things she said, it was the things I saw her do. It was how she lived her life in front of me. I learned by example. Prior to my health challenge, I had career goals, as I have already explained. But it was when I could no longer take life for granted, when I was told that I did not have long to live, that I wanted to live more than ever. I wanted something greater to live for than professional accomplishments, material assets, or career acclaim. I wanted to find greatness within myself. I no longer wanted to be "normal," average, or easily identifiable. I wanted to make a spiritual connection within myself that would enable me to mount up as an eagle and spread my wings as never before.

My mother is the one who laid the foundation in me that with God all things are possible! She was on life support 21 times that I can remember. I was overwhelmed the one time I was on life support. Each time she came away from those experiences, she always testified about how good God is. She never lost her faith. I understand more clearly at this stage of life, that her prayers and love for God made her a resilient woman. Little did I know how grateful I would be to her once I became older and faced my own life-threatening health challenges. As I was reflecting, it was her level of wisdom that she passed to me, giving me strength to learn how to fight. She was a living example of how to encourage yourself in times of adversities. Quite remarkably, just as I've been blessed to have my husband stand by me, my mother was also blessed to have had my father stand by her.

I challenge you to identify the true mentor or mentors in your life. This is a pleasant exercise that calls for reflection. Once you identify who those individuals are, you will feel a deep sense of gratitude rise up in you. You will you suddenly realize you were overlooking the living treasure God has placed in your midst. You will realize how blessed you are on a higher level. Why? Because your icons are your guardian angels. They are those special people that God has placed in your life who will make the greatest difference when the going gets tough. Just when you feel you cannot go on another day, much less another month, you will remember what your mentor taught you.

You will find yourself in a place of solitude once your pity party is over and all the excuses for giving up have gone home. Inside your own head, it will be your icons that you will draw from for strength, solace, and the will to live. When the chips are down and we decide not to stay down, it is our icons who will give us the courage to draw from their experiences and cause us to win in the end! When we must take action and overcome threats to our lives, our health, our marriage, our finances, or anything else, we need to reflect upon the actions of those people who successfully overcame the odds and lived to talk about it. In other words, we want to pattern ourselves after those who not only talk the talk but walk the walk.

My mother was just such a person: she walked the walk. She followed up her decisions with action. She was one of the reasons why I am where I am today. It is because of my mother that I found the courage to learn how to live again regardless

How Would You Look Back On Your Life?

of the life-threatening illness. In the process, I found a new and improved "me," and I am alive to talk about it!

It is because I had a mentor in my life who placed a seed of faith in me and deposited a deep and abiding faith in God that I have not only learned how to live again but changed my adversities into adventures.

To God be the glory!

Learn to rejoice—God can use your story for His glory!

FINDING YOUR PERFECT PARTNER: YOU

I learned how to become my own best friend by spending time with myself. Through soul-searching, I came to the realization that many times throughout my life, I had loved others and done more things for them than I would do for myself.

Thank God that this is a struggle of the past and not my destiny. Surely, I enjoy being me! I think I am awesome, and I've learned to take care of myself.

Regardless of age, we are beautiful because God made us beautiful creatures. But the world has conditioned us differently and set its own standards for classifying what beauty is. Many of us have bought into that way of thinking, and consequently, we have become discontented with ourselves, questioning whether we measure up to the world's standard.

It is important for every person to have a good and healthy relationship with themselves. Do you? No other person can complete you because they are not God. We should be comfortable in our own skin and not sink into the expectation that someone else needs to fix us or fill the void in our lives.

Although I was married for 40 years and enjoyed the companionship of my husband, I also enjoyed my own company. I realized that there is great value within me as an individual. Many of the adventures that I embarked upon, I did so without my husband. My husband had no problem telling me, "This is not what I want to do," and I had no problem with it either. He never discouraged me from doing what I wanted; he encouraged me to be myself. He took photos of me and cheered me on.

How Would You Look Back On Your Life?

We respected one another. He enjoyed watching me perform my adventures, and I got a thrill putting on a show. It worked well for us. After so many years of marriage, he let me do me, and I let him do him. We were whole people as individuals, and therefore, we embraced each other's uniqueness. We found the perfect partner in each other as a couple and the ideal partner in ourselves as individuals.

The most important relationship is the one we build with ourselves. Do you have an authentic relationship with yourself? If so, it is something you must be proud of, as being in touch with who you are will also enable you to build healthier relationships with others. It will decrease the stress on the other individual, so they do not become overwhelmed with the relationship. It does not matter whether it's a partner, a family member, or a friend—no one should bear the burden of trying to complete another person. I've known people whose behavior indicated they wanted me to fix their life. They would pull me into areas I didn't want to be in, and eventually, I became burned out with the relationship.

Once you learn that it is okay to be by yourself, give yourself some "me time." Resist the need for another person to validate or complete you, and it will become more enjoyable to spend time alone. I assure you, you don't want toxic people hanging around just because you want to be around someone. It helps if you appreciate who you are.

It is great to have good friends in life, but it is better to become your own best friend first. I have learned first-hand that it takes a lot of time to really get to know myself. By getting to know myself, I discovered reserves of strength in areas of life that I was not aware of.

How Would You Look Back On Your Life?

Sometimes, we have many hidden issues that we have not yet addressed, so we must get to know those parts of ourselves and take care of our mental health and well-being. It does not matter whether you are alone or with someone. We must dive deep within to understand ourselves before we can evaluate and get to know someone else.

As a woman of color, I dealt with many stigmas growing up. I was treated as if I were a second-class citizen. In my younger years, this affected my self-esteem. Often, I thought that I was not good enough, no matter how hard I tried. In that phase of my life, I was a product of my environment. However, I decided not to subscribe to those stigmas any longer. As you mature in life, you'll learn that you're a product of your decisions, not your environment.

The only person you will be with for the rest of your life is you. Everyone else is subject to leave one way or another. So, since you are the only person guaranteed to be with you, why not embrace yourself?

When you learn to be content and happy with yourself, you will be a joy to be around. You will also attract a healthier approach to relationships. If you struggle with the concept of being alone, know that you can learn to enjoy your own company if you give yourself the opportunity. The more you get to know and appreciate yourself, the less tolerance and patience you will find to deal with nonsense from others. You will be okay in your own skin. If you realize that you don't enjoy your own company, why not find your perfect partner now?

How Would You Look Back On Your Life?

Learn how to become your perfect partner by becoming comfortable in your own skin.

REKINDLE THE CHILD IN YOU

I don't buy into the philosophy of others that you should act your age. I remember when my husband first insisted that I sit on top of a luggage cart at the airport. I told him, "No way," several times. I thought it was such a silly idea. Finally, after all his coercing, I gave in. I was definitely not ready for what unfolded after that. He ran down the walkway with me, hanging on for dear life like a devilish boy. To say that I felt ashamed was an understatement. Here we were, two seasoned adults, acting like kids. I did wonder if others thought that we were out of our minds or merely going through a midlife crisis. Eventually, though, I looked forward to our new routine at the airport: getting on top of the luggage cart each time we traveled. Both of us would act like teenagers in our own world without worrying about what others thought. Looking back, I am grateful I got to enjoy such a fantastic experience every time I traveled with my husband. I would only focus on having fun. I felt like a playful kid each time we would do this, and it added so much spice to our traveling adventures and enhanced our adult lives. I'm learning how to recapture those childish feelings again.

Gregory was more of a child at heart than me. It took a little while, but I eventually learned to embrace and love the child in me. I would not want it any other way. We became happier people. Trust me; sometimes laughter makes life easier, more fun, and less stressful.

Playing on the floor with my grandchildren rekindled my curiosity to see the world from their perspective. Laughing and playing elicited feelings of fun and happiness in me and fed my soul. Children see their future as something filled with endless possibilities. No one is better at being a kid than kids themselves. Playing with them gave me the permission to act like a child. I began to enjoy watching kids' movies with them while lying on the floor, eating popcorn, and giggling along with them.

By embracing and indulging the child in you—which is the part of you that is more cheerful, optimistic, creative, and carefree—you will feel happier in life. For me, it helped me release some of the stress and focus on what was really important. Not only do I enjoy embracing my inner child, but I also love acting as one at times, especially when playing with my grandchildren. When I take my grandkids to the park, I enjoy playing on some of the equipment. Swinging on the swing helps me remember the carefree days of my own childhood. Thank God I that am less concerned about social pressures and can embrace the child in me.

How Would You Look Back On Your Life?

In this season of life, I feel younger than ever before. I believe the longer you can stay young in spirit, the longer you will feel mentally and physically younger. Whenever we enjoy life, engage in playfulness, exhibit curiosity and fearlessness, are open to meet new people, desire to go to new places, and try to start new projects—everything that younger people usually do—we stay young at heart.

Adults laugh fewer than 15 times per day, but kids laugh over 300 times per day. As part of learning not to make every aspect of my life seem so serious, I joined a Laughter Yoga group. It is said that 20 minutes of laughter can have a profound effect on your health and well-being. There are times I laugh so hard that it becomes hard to breathe; I start coughing and sometimes gasp for air. I don't allow the coughing sensation to stop me from laughing, though. Adding laughter to my life has allowed me to feel great and live in the moment instead of focusing on my problems.

Laughter also boosts your immune system. So, I do plenty of laughing to help mine. Moreover, it also helps you stay physically and mentally resilient. It increases oxygen intake and provides an energy boost to make you feel alive.

How Would You Look Back On Your Life?

As someone who is now a child at heart, I believe in manifesting the laughing practice into action. One night, I served as a hostess at a sarcoidosis fundraising event. My job was to make the guests feel comfortable. During this event, I glanced across the room and saw a tall man with a giant yellow snake wrapped around his shoulders and neck. I realized this was a part of the entertainment aspect of the event. He was parading around the entire room. Anyone who knows me is aware of how petrified I am of snakes. The very sight of one would make my flesh crawl.

I started freaking out and then realized that I had to maintain my composure. I did not want to end up on any social media platform, screaming and acting crazy. I had to practice self-talk effectively during this time. I kept telling myself, "Keep it moving, Dorothy. When the man and snake move to one side of the room, you move to the other. Just keep your eyes on him, and you will be fine, girl."

I glanced at the mirror and began to laugh at myself. I looked like a scared child moving around the room as I looked over my shoulders like a thief while dodging a man with a snake. Instead of getting embarrassed, I laughed at myself. By laughing at myself, I felt less stressed and more relaxed.

It was working. As time went on, ironically, intrigue began to set in. I started feeling more comfortable and began mingling with a small group of women. We were all laughing and having fun. Suddenly, from the corner of my eye, I noticed that the man with the snake was standing behind me. I froze and was unable to move. As if that wasn't enough, one of the ladies in front of me shouted to the guy, "Let her hold it!" If I was in my right mind, I think I would have choked her.

In a deep voice, the man said, "Close your eyes." Since I was in a trance, I closed my eyes out of fear.

He laid that snake on my shoulder. It was so heavy that my legs started to wobble. Next, he said, "Give me your hand." Then he went on to put the snake's head in my hand. When I came to myself, I screamed, "JESUS!!" I was holding a hundred-pound yellow boa constrictor around my body. If that wasn't bad enough, the head of the snake whipped around and stared at me, straight into my eyes. I stood there feeling helpless and in disbelief that this was happening to me. In a very short time, I came out of my trance and realized that the music was playing. The snake was still wrapped around me, and we were looking at each other, eye to eye. I began to move along with the music. All of a sudden, the snake didn't look so bad to me. Can you believe that I started dancing and laughing with my new partner? It might sound somewhat weird, but it felt good to be able to laugh at myself during this event and to be able to reminisce about it later.

In the past, I felt vulnerable when I was fearful. Now I can allow myself to see the humor in situations. People around me also laughed with me as I went from being scared stiff to partying with this yellow boa. I still laugh about this incident when I look at the photos.

I learned that laughing at myself is healthy. People are far too serious about themselves because they want to establish and maintain a specific image. The reality is that we're all flawed and simply can't be perfect all the time. Remember that God has given us the amazing gift of laughter. The Word of God says, *"A merry heart does good like medicine"* (Proverbs 17:22). Boy, did I get a big dose of medication that night laughing! I am an imperfect human being with many flaws. So, I have learned how to laugh at myself in the midst of my flaws and fears.

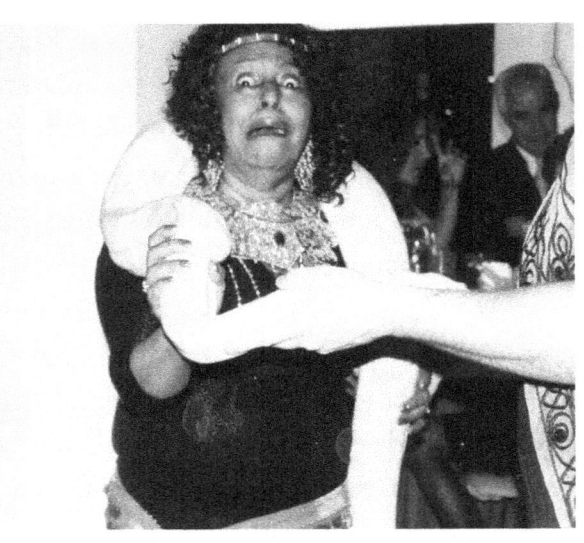

How Would You Look Back On Your Life?

Learn how to conquer your fears.
There is so much joy and a sense of freedom
in being able to laugh at yourself.
Learn to give yourself permission to be carefree,
have fun and rekindle the child in you.

IV

Keeping Your Adventurous Self Alive

In finding myself, surviving this ordeal, and coming to life again, I decided that adventure was no longer a luxury but an obligation to myself. I decided to squeeze every glorious drop of life out of my time. I went crazy in experiencing life, drinking from the cup, and spotting the beauty and wonder in everything has now become a habit.

In trying to find where the limits are, I discovered it was the sky... by literally jumping out of a plane. Yes, that's correct, I did a tandem jump from a perfectly functional plane at 14,000 feet. I jumped right out of it. As I jumped from the plane, my breath was caught in my throat, in a completely different manner from the beginning of my story. I was terrified and delighted all at once, and when the roaring, endless fall turned into a silent and awe-inspiring float down to the earth, I knew there was no place I would be closer to God. I could watch small specks of cars crawling across the landscape, the glint of the sun across metal objects in the distance, the earth given to us by the grace of God. Why had I been so afraid to courageously explore this wholesome beauty at any opportunity I could?

I have a list of amazing experiences under my belt, each more exciting than the last. Some were successful, some not, but man, am I happy that I decided to open those doors. Not only did I explore adventurous activities, but I doubled it up with international travel. I rappelled down 27 stories for the Respiratory Health Association at a hotel in downtown Chicago; I did the extreme zip line in Costa Rica; I rode an elephant in Thailand and a camel in Egypt.

The greatest achievement for anyone would be to live an exciting, adventurous life unapologetically, so you will have no regrets in the end. That's what matters. Now is the best time to begin living! Sometimes you must ask yourself, "Am I doing what makes me happy? When will I start doing me? What feels exciting and adventurous to me?"

I remember making the decision to begin the greatest adventure of my life by writing a list of activities that excited my inner adventurous self. I wanted to experience what it would feel like to come out of my comfort zone and position myself in these adventures while challenging myself to truly live for me. At least once in my life, I wanted to be able to say, "Yes! I experienced that!" Now, here I am, willing to share these moments with you. I have discovered my true self, and you can too! It is never too late for you to become fearlessly adventurous while you are still breathing.

Keeping Your Adventurous Self Alive

I thank God that my late husband, Gregory, was by my side through most of my adventures. He was my biggest supporter, my loudest cheerleader, and the photographer who captured every memorable moment. Although he would cheer me on, I can hear him saying, "Baby! You do you, but I'm going to keep my feet on the ground!" He would say, "I have no intentions on jumping out of a plane at this stage of my life." He did share some adventurous activities with me. I'm so thankful for the support I had from him encouraging me to "do me," and for all the wonderful adventures we experienced together.

Learn to find a way to keep your adventurous self alive.
As long as you have life, there is an adventure in you.

LEARNING TO LIVE AGAIN IN THE MIDST OF LIFE CIRCUMSTANCES

After you see the light at the end of your tunnel, there are some things that can throw you back into a tailspin. It's hard to grasp what just happened. You become confused and lost in dealing with the new circumstance.

My husband, Gregory, made his transition in November 2017. I miss my best friend, confidant, and travel buddy. I'm thankful to God for giving us all the glorious memories we had together. The pictures and videos of the vacations and adventures we shared still bring me so much joy. I miss his infectious laughter and silly jokes, and the way he was always telling me, "Yes, dear," as though he agreed with me, but it was only to shut me up.

Keeping Your Adventurous Self Alive

My husband was blessed to be surrounded by love and comfort from our children, grandchildren, and close family members. We all witnessed him taking his last breath. I heard our children crying and screaming in agony. There was no weeping in my voice. I was too stunned, feeling as though I was dreaming.

After losing my husband within two weeks of his prognosis, I was in a state of confusion and denial for nearly a year. Although I was going through life's motions daily, it didn't hit me until his birthday almost a year later. This was when the most challenging part of my grieving hit. For a while, I felt I couldn't move. Grief had drained my energy. I couldn't believe Greg was gone. Although I had strong support from my children, who continually checked in on me to ensure I was okay, it didn't fill the void of not having their dad there with me.

I was literally walking around in a daze. With the help of a dear friend, I was encouraged to join a bereavement support group. It's good to know that you do not have to walk through the valley alone. By sharing stories with others, problems become less fearsome. Receiving comfort and encouragement from others who were experiencing similar circumstances helped me feel that I was not alone. It was not easy for me to share in the beginning because I was still dealing with the shock of the sudden loss of my husband. The valuable educational and emotional support helped me to cope better with my current circumstance.

After having been a part of the support group for over a year, I started feeling stronger psychologically. I shared that we were avid travelers who explored over 20 countries on five continents together. We journeyed to Egypt's pyramids, the Pantheon of Rome, China's Great Wall, and so many other places. I also shared that we had celebrated 40 years of marriage.

Keeping Your Adventurous Self Alive

After going through the grieving process and much prayer, I decided to cherish the wish we had for one another. I realized that I still had so much to be thankful for during my loss, pain, and heartache, like the years we spent together raising a family. I'm glad we made memories of those years of marriage. Dealing with his passing caused me to redefine my life and continue to carry out our wish to continue living in the other's absence. In the midst of this new life circumstance, I have had to learn to live again and turn my recent adversity into more adventures.

Gregory would always say, "Dorothy, let's make some memories." And boy, did we! Years later, I am still enjoying all of the memories we made together.

I had to renew my perspective to survive my ordeal of losing my spouse. I gained strength from knowing how blessed I was to have someone love me unconditionally. Eventually, I changed my perception of my husband's loss and focused on how fortunate I was. God is still with me, and I had to remember His presence. When I think about God's goodness, it gives me strength.

Yes, I miss all the jokes Gregory would tell me. His famous saying to me, "Dorothy, you're head and shoulders above the rest," was his way of lifting my spirits. I'm glad we had conversations about our wishes for after the transition for the one who is left behind.

Losing my husband suddenly was earth-shattering, life-altering, and indescribably painful. But I have learned to live again in the midst of it. Now, my focus is on thanking God for blessing my marriage for those 40 years. I feel so blessed that I had such a caring and compassionate husband, not only with our children and me but also with many other family members.

Keeping Your Adventurous Self Alive

I decided to revisit Havana, Cuba, which was my husband's dream vacation. Going back gave me comfort in reminiscing our time spent together there.

No matter what your life circumstances are, you will thrive again. I cannot tell you when, as it's different for everyone, but you will. Until then, breathe. It's the only thing you have to do at this moment. Breathe during your circumstances, and don't forget to pray and exercise your faith.

Keeping Your Adventurous Self Alive

Learn not to lose hope regardless of what you are going through in the midst of life circumstances.

DEVELOP A NEW YOU

Developing a new me was the beginning of a new chapter in my life; I am now writing a new story of a new version of myself. Although I am the same person, I have a new identity. I was called Mrs. Williams for most of my adult life. Now, I have a new

Keeping Your Adventurous Self Alive

identity. I'm no longer Mrs. Williams, a wife. I had to venture out and rediscover myself as a widow, a single individual.

After my husband passed away, I experienced real heartbreak. I remembered Gregory saying, "If something happens to me first, I want you to continue to live." We both expressed the same wish for one another. When he died, though, all of the previous talks went out the window for a while. My whole life felt like it had been turned upside down. Everything was so new to me. The adjustment didn't go so well. I experienced a lot of anxiety, sleepless nights, and loss of appetite. I was in disbelief that he was gone so suddenly.

My bereavement support group helped me heal from pain and grief. It gave me encouragement, helpful advice, and hope. I felt a sense of normalcy while attending, knowing that I was not going through my ordeal alone. It gave me a sense of freedom to express my feelings and talk to others about the loss of my husband. This was my first step to healing.

Eventually, I gained the feeling of hope that I could rebuild my life in some positive way. Since I was now single for the first time in years and my children were all adults, I felt like I needed to get to see myself in a different light. Taking the time to reflect allowed me to rethink being single. I wanted to learn new ways to improve myself, and what I really wanted to do in life became my focus.

My awareness that my time here on earth is limited has been heightened. I have discovered that satisfying thirst for the next adventure has become a priority in my life.

Everyone handles losses differently, and there is no set way to do it. I knew my husband did not want me to give up on life.

Keeping Your Adventurous Self Alive

My first year without him was mass confusion, so I made no drastic changes, but then I slowly started to change as circumstances forced me into a new lifestyle of singleness. I made an effort to keep moving so I would not get stuck in my grief and allow it to find a home in my soul.

At this stage of my life, I became accustomed to stepping out of my comfort zone to keep growing in my new independence. It helps to learn to be comfortable with being uncomfortable. I grasped this concept thoroughly and took that leap of faith once again. Now that I was single, I had to tap into another version of myself, the new me. It took some time to get used to this new norm in my life.

Although I enjoy the company of others, I have learned how to do things alone. I felt the need to adjust to the new norm of becoming single after 40 years of marriage. I was accustomed to traveling with my husband, but I realized that I must step out of my box again and continue to fulfill my dreams. I started going out alone to breakfast and dinner, opera and plays, sitting by the lake, and other activities I enjoyed. My first solo trip was back to Cuba. It felt great to recapture the moments that my husband and I spent together there. I stayed at the same hotel and recognized some of the people we had met before.

Initially, I struggled with the idea of being alone, and I was forced to let myself learn to love my own company and not allow the fear of being uncomfortable to discourage me from doing so. Instead, in this new season of becoming a widow, it became a catalyst for growth.

I loved my husband dearly, and I wish he were here with me. But now, I've learned how to move forward and realized I must make plans for my future.

Keeping Your Adventurous Self Alive

When I faced my illness, I didn't give up, and now I'm applying the same mentality so that I won't give up living in the midst of my new circumstances. I am hoping to continue to be my adventurous self.

After I started living my life to the fullest, I wrote down activities that I felt like I needed to experience at least once in my life. I have now made a new list of activities on my bucket list that I wouldn't mind doing alone. These things not only impress my inner adventurous self, but they also represent me getting out of my comfort bubble to become single. Traveling was familiar terrain, so I have continued that journey. I started to travel again without feeling out of place. By reinventing myself, I have developed a new me!

Keeping Your Adventurous Self Alive

Learn to be your own best friend and develop a new you.

THE TIME TO LIVE UNAPOLOGETICALLY IS NOW!

There is a saying, "If you make friends with yourself, you will never be alone." I started enjoying my own company. In this season of my life, I have felt freer than ever before; I discovered the real me and embraced the new girl! She loves adventures, is willing to take risks, and doesn't mind stepping out of her box. She is an overcomer and a playful little girl on the inside. She no longer cares about what others think of her. Now she is living to be true to herself. She no longer fits into the societal model of conformity that tells her how she should be at a given age. She embraces and celebrates her uniqueness and loves every minute of it unapologetically!

Keeping Your Adventurous Self Alive

My experience in life has shaped me to become the individual I am today. I give thanks to Him for molding me into this new woman.

Living unapologetically didn't come naturally for me. It was gradual as I became more of a seasoned adult and had a better understanding of myself. In my former years, I would apologize for everything, even if it was not my fault. The negative words I said took a foothold in my life, making me feel insecure and less than who I was. I don't allow those words to resonate in my spirit any longer, because I now know who I am. I have learned how to love who I am and not apologize when I don't live up to others' expectations. This is the new me. I'm still making plenty of mistakes in life, but I'm learning how to give myself grace and not beat myself up as I have done in the past.

Living unapologetically can be defined as a deep feeling of freedom: living your best self without approval and taking a stand for your mental, physical, and spiritual well-being; being true to yourself and letting go of what everyone else is saying. I have learned to treat and pamper myself and not feel guilty about it. It feels good to have the courage to step outside of my comfort zone to do what I enjoy. There was a period in my life when I felt compelled to say "yes" to keep from hurting other people's feelings. This stemmed from years of conditioning that I received during my formative years. To briefly elaborate, I was taught that saying "no" was rude. That bondage mindset is no longer a trait of my character nor a part of my life. Now that I respect my feelings, I possess the capability of saying no unapologetically. Being myself allows me the freedom of expression to do the things I like. I grew up not having a voice, but I don't allow myself to feel insecure any longer for not pleasing others.

People care about what others think, because it is only natural. But there is a way to stay balanced and stay true to who you are at the same time. You must have the freedom to be who you really are and not feel like you must be like anyone else.

After going through the experience of my life, I can embrace the real me with all my flaws and imperfections. It's okay, because there are no perfect human beings on the face of this earth. Traveling to different countries has also taught me how to embrace other people's uniqueness, celebrate their culture, and respect their beliefs and traditions. Almighty God has made each of us unique; all our fingerprints are different. I've learned not to judge other people because of the differences in our lifestyles, philosophy of life, or beliefs. Meeting and learning about other individuals on my travels has enriched my world and opened my eyes to so many possibilities. I've grown to appreciate what life has to offer.

I have been working on being unapologetic about who I am and what I'm doing with my life. It's my life, and I choose to live it on my terms. Sometimes, we apologize out of habit. It's time to stop! To live unapologetically, one of the most important places to start is getting to know the real you. Remember to find your perfect partner, which is you. Embrace who you are and celebrate your uniqueness rather than trying to please others and fit in or feeling like you have to conform to anyone else's lifestyle. Be you; don't fit in someone else's mold to be accepted by others. Be true to yourself, stop trying to fit in or conform, and don't allow others to tell you how you should look or who you should be. Embrace your own uniqueness. If you don't, then eventually, you will lose the ability to be your authentic self.

I love the woman I have become. I have learned to step outside my box and truly be myself. I now enjoy life on my own terms, and I have learned how to rise above the challenges in my life.

Keeping Your Adventurous Self Alive

I challenge you to stop wasting your time on other people's opinions about you. Your future is not predicated on someone else. Be bold and stand up for yourself, and don't be afraid to say "no" to things that just aren't right for you. Don't spend the rest of your life trying to change others' opinions of you, because their opinion really doesn't matter. You owe no one your peace of mind, nor an explanation for being you. Be sure to take the time frequently to do something only for yourself. Don't deprive yourself by not fulfilling your dreams.

Today, I am no longer making others comfortable at my own expense. I spend time with the people who love me for who I am. I enjoy doing things I love, and I live my life and my dreams without apology.

Learn to be true to who you are.
Be your own biggest supporter.

NEW PERSPECTIVE IN LIFE

A change in perspective is more than just a change in your opinions about important issues. A true change in your perspective can lead you into making life-altering decisions that may result in new experiences, new friends, and a new level of awareness about the world around you. In other words, you will begin to have a positive impact on the world as a result of your change in perspective triggered by a change in consciousness. You are changing not only from the inside out, but also from the outside in.

When I gained a new perspective in life, I altered my posture. I suppressed my opponents who tried to stop me from living my dream because they were afraid to step out of their own box. I started creating a better future and started living life more fully in the moment. Boy, did I start having more fun! It is never a waste to change your story in life. It all begins with a new perspective on how you see yourself in your story, and whether you are happy with it or decide to rewrite your script and begin a new journey.

I no longer live by the old script of playing it safe in most areas of my life, as I did in my past. People had projected their fears onto me, but I realized they were not my own. My self-perception is no longer feeling like a victim of circumstance, but knowing that I am a victor over it.

I'm not resistant to changes, because for me, it's all about growth. When I gained a new perspective in life, I was able to accept the new changes. When I travel, I am able to explore new territory. I often watched the Travel Channel, but that second-hand experience can't compare to actually being there to experience it. It takes on an entirely different meaning. My horizons and perspective broadened, which caused me to look at life and people differently.

Keeping Your Adventurous Self Alive

Sometimes we can become stuck with our way of life and forget that there are alternative ways of living—there's more than just one way to do things. We can discover new realities. When I travel to a new country, I leave my judgment behind and come with an open mind to learn and embrace the country's uniqueness. I love listening to others share about their culture because it gives me a new perspective on life. Also, it allows me to learn about their differences, similarities, and religious values.

As I learned how to live again as a widow, I ventured to South Africa. I experienced several safaris, which was one of my dream vacations. My experience was so incredible. Seeing all the animals in their natural habitat close up and first-hand was thrilling.

I never did so much dancing before I started traveling. While I was dancing with the natives in Africa, they showed me their moves, and I burst out into my own moves. Their commonality was laughter, fun, and having a great time together. No judgment toward one another, just sharing the happiness.

Experiencing this travel adventure was like being in a euphoric state of mind. I felt like I was on cloud nine. I appreciated finding myself in a new place, as though I had reached another plateau in life. When God elevates us to higher heights, it's a powerful feeling. It is a spiritual high that nothing else can rival. My deep-seated desire to get more out of living as a single individual was the catalyst for reinforcing my positive attitude toward living.

What would it look like if you were to build conditions in the present moment that will free you from your past? Despite my adversities, I could testify to how good God had been to me. God blessed me to live and allowed me to have another opportunity to start all over again with a new attitude. My gain did not grow out of my losses, but my losses made room for new blessings.

Keeping Your Adventurous Self Alive

Traveling has given me many unforgettable and mesmerizing experiences. On my trip to South Africa, I joined a group of people from different regions of the United States. It was an eye-opening experience for me and an incredibly educational one too. I gained unique insight, new knowledge, and new perspectives on the culture. I tried many new foods, listened to new music, met new people, saw new sites, and experienced so many new things. I even rekindled my dancing spirit to the music of the culture.

One way to change your viewpoint on life is to associate yourself with different groups of people, by which I mean diverse cultures. With time, you get used to the diversity of views and thoughts, and you can benefit from other cultures. This diversity of perspective allows you to receive insight on which to base your new vision of reality. Different people can help us see things we would otherwise not see, and they can present opportunities we otherwise wouldn't consider. Meeting new people from various parts of the globe is a perfect way to share different approaches with people from other cultures.

To get a new perspective on life, we need to decide today to do something differently from yesterday. People from poor and conflict-ridden countries can help us understand how blessed we are, and this should never be taken for granted. When I visited Africa, I experienced that many of the people were content with what they had and full of joy. Can you imagine not having your basic needs met, or not having something essential such as suitable housing or clean water available to you? I experienced an inner connectedness while in Africa. I experienced myself awakening to its natural, cultural, and historical richness; a belief in its potential to thrive; and its diversified unity as one continent.

When we gain a new perspective, the world becomes more exciting and beautiful. An atmosphere of harmony seems to fill our surroundings. It often makes the difference in whether you resist or accept the new changes that are happening in your life.

My perspective toward life has enabled me to envision a new me. Since we have the power to change our story or our path in life, I declared that my story was not over. I had a lot of living to do.

Learn how to explore other options to enhance your spirit, which may help you to develop a different perspective in life.

PERSONAL TRANSFORMATION AND GROWTH

It was vital for me to understand that my challenges were part of my growth in life. Without them, I would not be the person I am today, because I have been molded into a stronger individual. Radical changes happen most of the time out of desperation, which is what occurred in my case.

Now, I have a driving force within me to keep going regardless of my circumstances. God says the renewing of our mind will transform us (Romans 12:2). I learned I must exercise this ability He invested within me.

There is nothing as powerful as a changed mind. You can change your outward aspects, like physical appearance, clothing, hair, friends, and residence, but if you don't change your mind, the same experience will repeat itself. You see, only the external stuff changes, but nothing inward does. People struggling with challenges each face essentially the same set of problems and fears, but with their own individual coping styles. My growth through my transformation enabled me to better handle the adversities that come in my life because of my prior experience and a changed mind.

As a part of my morning ritual to set the spirit for my day, I awake with gratitude. I'm thankful to be alive, to have healthy children, to be able to breathe, to have a home, to have beautiful memories of my husband, and the list goes on and on. I have learned to give thanks for the simple blessings of the day.

Gratitude can help to improve your overall attitude. Begin to be grateful for what you have right now and what you have had, even if you no longer have it. When you practice this attitude, you will notice a beautiful change in your life. Your perception of yourself will undoubtedly improve.

Although my husband is not physically present with me, I have continued living my life while discovering my adventurous self. Today, I continually grow and transform myself as a single individual. As long as we are present here on earth, no matter what age, we should make room for growth and find time to enjoy living. Eventually, you will notice a transformation in yourself.

I have been given the opportunity to become a facilitator or presenter at various health support groups. I share my health challenges on these platforms to encourage and empower other individuals who are also experiencing their own personal health challenges. As a result of my experience, I am a firm believer that people who suffer from a critical illness deserve more emotional support than they are receiving from the medical establishment. God has been so good in my life that I try to pay it forward by becoming a blessing to build and uplift people with similar challenges.

My health challenge journey has also led me to become an advocate with the Respiratory Health Association (RHA) in Chicago. The RHA's mission is to prevent lung disease, promote clean air, and help people live better through education, research, and policy change. This mission has given me an outlet to demonstrate my passion and enthusiasm to advocate for lung health and share my story. I have traveled to Springfield, Illinois, many times and recruited others to support lung health initiatives as part of the RHA's State Lung Health Education Day. Also, I have met with federal legislators in Washington, D.C., about issues related to lung health, and I've supported the RHA at congressional and environmental meetings to help advance its mission.

During my transformation and growth season, I decided to push myself to another level by taking part in a summer bike ride with the RHA called CowaLUNGa. I thought, what better way to add another adventure to my bucket list and also join with other people to support a great cause that is dear to my heart.

My passion and determination for the cause to raise money for lung health made me go the extra distance. Instead of doing only 18 miles, which was the shortest distance offered, I went for the gusto, a three-day bike ride of 190 miles. I was determined to make it happen. On my birthday, my family brought me a lightweight bike to ensure that I had the right type of bike to participate in this event. I only had five months to prepare. My determination was the driving force for me to practice riding daily. I was very excited to be an actual participant and not just a spectator in this event.

There is a certain rewarding feeling inside when what you are doing can be beneficial to other people. As the event started, we started pedaling and moving forward along the route. I did not feel any pressure to keep up with anyone. I put my headphones on to listen to some inspirational music and started my journey.

When riding became a bit challenging, I would rest. When I faced a steep slope, I would try to walk up with my bike or wait for a sag van to come and give me a ride. I had to ride an average of 65 miles per day. I can honestly say that it was quite challenging, and I put forth all my effort to complete this race. When the third day finally came, I was pretty exhausted. Wow! What determination will do!

Keeping Your Adventurous Self Alive

Thank God I no longer allow circumstances to define me or place limitations on my life. To overcome adversity, you must develop a healthy state of mind. Thank God I learned to keep the tenacity of refusing to give up in many situations in my life. I wouldn't allow my circumstances to direct my path. My only option was to hold fast to my dreams and vision. Today, I still advocate for the Respiratory Health Association and continue to stay positive throughout my journey.

I am growing so much in this season. It excites me when I can look back on my growth and see the progression that I've made. I've been able to create these new norms for myself, even after the loss of my husband and the hardship I have experienced. Again, I learned to step outside of my box into a new venue of life.

Learn how to take on a new challenge.

My transformation has helped me to grow in many areas of overcoming fear. One great example is that I decided to do rappelling with the Respiratory Health Association's annual fundraising event. I rappelled down 27 stories at a hotel in downtown Chicago. It may look like I was having fun, but initially, I was scared to death from looking down alone. My imagination was going wild with fear. The most challenging part was to lean over the edge and take the first step to start rappelling down the building.

It took over an hour to convince myself to go through with it. Other participants kept encouraging me and assuring me that I would do fine. I signed up for it, that meant I had to go through with it.

Rappelling is something that I had never done before, so it further raised my curiosity. The safety harness was definitely tight. There were all types of crazy thoughts racing through my head, like "What if I lose my balance and hit my head on the glass?"

Then I remembered that God has not given me a spirit of fear. I started saying my affirmations: *I am brave enough to take chances. I can do all things through Christ who strengthens me. I am a conqueror. I am strong and powerful.* Every strength-building affirmation I could think of, I said.

Why did I look down? Oh my goodness, the chilling sensation that engulfed my soul. Still, I needed to overcome my fears sooner rather than later, so I tried my best to contain myself. With some pre-preparation, I finally mustered up the nerve to lean backward on that 27-story building.

Once I did it, it wasn't so bad, so I began to proceed down with the first step to start rappelling down the building. I started feeling very fretful again because I was losing control in maintaining my balance due to the glass windows, which made my feet continuously slide off the glass.

Keeping Your Adventurous Self Alive

I tried my best to maintain my grip and stay in the rhythm walking down, slow and steady. Halfway down, I heard my family cheering me on, chanting many words of encouragement. "You got this!" "Go, mama, go!" What a boost of confidence.

I broke out in a dance called the wobble, shaking my hips from side to side. I felt like a kid again at that moment. This whole rappelling process was pretty tricky for me. Still, I somehow managed to finally reach ground level with my family and other spectators cheering for me.

Overcoming my transformation of fear has enabled me to become a bolder individual.

Keeping Your Adventurous Self Alive

Learn to be bold and not let fear hold you back.
Transform into the person God intends for you to be.

ADVENTURES DURING THE COVID-19 SEASON

The Covid-19 season has been unlike anything we have ever experienced, and many of us are missing people we lost since 2020. Now is the time when we begin to move forward, not back to what was, but shaping what we want the world to be in the future.

Keeping Your Adventurous Self Alive

I realized that during those seasons of testing in my life, God was working something in me. Now I'm able to step out of situations that are not my norm and trust God regardless.

Covid-19 became the new reality of living. I didn't panic about all the changes in the social norms. It only caused me to step out in faith and stay obedient to God's word. One thing life has taught me is that I'm not in control of it when the storms of life come. After all, I have faced so many, and I've learned to rely on my prayer, faith, and patience to bring me through.

I have learned that the only way to connect with God is through faith. Sometimes, our fears and disbeliefs hinder us from trusting beyond our comprehension. There were many days when my back was against the wall and the hurdles of life rose at me. I could have been counted out and not survived. The power of God kept springing in while I was going through these ordeals. Once I realized that the situations were out of my hands, my faith multiplied, making me a stronger believer in God's Word. My mind said, "This is a problem for God, so exercise your faith."

The Word of God says, *"We walk by faith and not by sight"* (2 Corinthians 5:7). I needed to trust God wholeheartedly in what I could not understand by pushing beyond my shaky thoughts and rattled feelings.

The leading cause of people's anxiety is the fear of the unknown. We want to obtain instant answers to all our questions, and when the answers don't meet our standards, worry and panic begin to set in. Just think about it: there has probably been a time when you were uncertain about something or did not know how it would turn out. How did you feel? You were probably feeling a little bit unsure and worried that the outcome would not be good. You probably went through various scenarios in your head

Keeping Your Adventurous Self Alive

about the possible results and then became worried that the worst-case scenario was the one you would have to deal with. In all likelihood, this is not the case. The scenario will work out fine, but people will still spend time getting worried and anxious about it. People of faith can override what they see naturally by trusting God fully in what they can't make sense of on their own.

During the Covid-19 season, when I discovered it was okay to be outside in the open air, my adventurous self was on! I still did adventurous activities safely, making sure I followed the CDC guidelines about practicing social distancing.

After being on top of the world, both literally and figuratively, I decided to choose more "grounded" activities in some of my other adventures. What came to my mind was enjoying nature. After searching and browsing the internet, I discovered many options: horseback riding, visiting different national parks, forest preserves, paddle boat, canoeing, go-cart racing, and golfing, to name a few. These activities excited me and stirred up my adventurous self again.

Two of my favorite activities were paddle boating and horseback riding. I've gone paddle boating several times during the Covid-19 season. The lake brought peace to my soul. Horseback riding in the forest was truly a wonderful experience. I relished all the amazing scenery.

Today, I still have many new adventures on my list to experience. As long as I have breath, I will try to keep living life adventurously with passion. I have learned not to allow situations to stop me from living my best life.

Keeping Your Adventurous Self Alive

Learn to move forward
instead of looking back to what was.

Keeping Your Adventurous Self Alive

REFLECTIONS ON MY ADVENTURES

I find it pretty amusing to reminisce on the times when I took all of my adventurous photos. These activities were some of the most challenging adventures I have experienced in my whole life. It was taxing, tedious, and demanding, but also thrilling, gratifying, and rewarding. I did not regret the time I spent pursuing these activities—not for even a single second.

When I came up with the idea of a bucket list, I simply thought of it as some sort of exercise to revitalize my will to keep living. And it did—and not only that, by doing these activities I have changed gradually as a person. I became courageous and pumped up for more action. Now I realize my journey does not have to stop here. My adventurous self that lay dormant for years was revived again and I have never felt younger.

You can find your own way to keep your adventurous self alive. You can start by observing other opportunities in your vicinity, and from there, start taking your leap of faith. You do not know how hard or easy it will be until you try it, so you might as well pack it up and get ready to go. This precious time that we have right now needs to be used accordingly. Make some stories about your journey that you can tell your children and grandchildren in the future, so that you can not only be proud of yourself, but also inspire others by sharing your experiences.

Let my journey be an example for you. You do not have to fly an airplane or experience driving a race car to be adventurous. By simply facing yourself and taking steps to get outside your box, you are already on the path to becoming more adventurous.

And from there, you will soar far above your fondest hopes and dreams.

V

Conclusion

In this book, I have shared my personal story of changing my adversities into adventures and learning to live again through my trials. For me, "Learning to Live Again" had to be the title of my book as well.

I have strived in these pages to send a message to you, my reader, that receiving bad news of any kind does not mean the end of the world, nor the end of your dreams. You can learn how to stir the adventure in you no matter what life sets across your path. Focusing on the positive side of a difficult situation is good for your mental and physical health.

Whatever your personal circumstances, I wrote this book to let you know, based on my own heart-wrenching experience, that you too can live adventurously on the heels of your adversity. I achieved many things by taking hope to a new level. During my

Conclusion

journey, I re-examined where my life was going. In the process, I redefined my goals and objectives. In so doing, thinking about living adventurously not only became feasible and obtainable, it also became a reality.

For me, my very physical life depended upon having the right attitude. My success was greatly dependent on my ability and determination to picture myself where I wanted to be. If I had imagined that I could not get well or that I would not live, my chances of living and getting well would have been greatly diminished. So, it cannot be about diagnosis, prognosis, or how much money you need but don't have. It has to be about the report you want to believe, and that report must be one that you write, compose, and construct for yourself. You must be the author of your own fate. When it comes to the process of writing your own report, you must put God first in order to avoid any negative reports you have received, regardless of your religion or belief system.

With faith and determination, life's difficulties do not become the measure of a man or woman, but rather their ability to survive with dignity. Most people, at some point in their lives, find themselves in a very bad place. What do I mean by this? Challenges come and life happens. Many things happen beyond our control. Faith is the key to believing that someone can get beyond where they are.

We take off the gloves when we learn to live again and turn our adversities into adventures. We unbutton our collar. We alter our posture. We dare to win. We have a new surge of energy. We kick doubt to the curb. We silence our critics. We begin to create a better future. We start living life more fully at that moment. We may even start having some fun. We are operating outside of

Conclusion

the box. We are exploring new territory. We are discovering new realities. We are creating a new course. We are looking at life and people differently. We are growing spiritually. We are creating a new image of ourselves. We are healing. We are generating a testimony! We no longer fear the unknown. We believe in ourselves. We believe we can fly. We know we will land safely and in a better place than the one we left behind.

Make no mistake, I am still on my journey. There is no ending. The journey only expands to take in more life, more liberty, and more joy. Once you learn how to live again and start turning your adversities into adventures, you may recognize the difference in yourself. Others will recognize a difference in you as well. It will be an expanded version of what you previously had to offer of yourself to others. As you change your adversities into victories, you will tap into more of your God-given potential. Now, you will be motivated as never before to reach your greatest potential. You will find that your impulses and instincts have become stronger. Why? Because your commitment to success has been heightened to a fever pitch!

So, don't wait for the right time. Now is the time to start *Learning to Live Again,* turning your *Adversities to Adventures,* and experiencing a conscious awakening of vast possibilities for the personal transformation and growth that you never thought was possible.

www.ingramcontent.com/pod-product-compliance
Lightning Source LLC
Chambersburg PA
CBHW062113080426
42734CB00012B/2852